My Depression . . .
My Survival to Overcome

My Depression ...
My Survival to Overcome

PAULINE MAGAUTA MOLOKWANE

PARTRIDGE

Print information available on the last page.

To order additional copies of this book, contact
Toll Free 0800 990 914 (South Africa)
+44 20 3014 3997 (outside South Africa)
orders.africa@partridgepublishing.com

www.partridgepublishing.com/africa

Contents

1. Introduction 1

2. Who I was. 6

3. My Story 82

4. I had to overcome. 112

5. My survival. 117

6. My goals to move on with my positive life 122

7. My personal poet and quotes to overcome my
   depression 126

8. Finding Myself 154

9. Acknowledgement 165

10. Biography 167

'God is good…all the time'

Dedication

2 Timothy 1:7

*God has not given us the spirit of fear, but
of boldness, love and sound mind"*

Every day we experience depression.
There are signs to look at and to
attend before it is too late..

I had to forgive myself first, I had to deal with my past emotional gaps, I had to prove it to myself than to the world. I had to forgive people who have hurt me in the past. I had to value my life, find my potential my gift and go back to God, have conversation with Him so that I can realise my purpose.

These questions challenged me during my Depression stage. Who am I? What I want? Where am I going? And what is my purpose?

I had to seek professional help and realize that fighting depression is a process. Psychologist will facilitate the healing process but it was my choice and had to make a decision to overcome the diagnosed depression. I had to feel that I have survived it and make possible to live a normal life without being seen as depressed person. Depression is dangerous; it has broken friendship, relationship, families and marriages. Depression has destroyed best companies. Depression can lead to suicidal if not dealt with at the early stage.

There are signs of depression, it is a slow poison but it will destroy you gradually when your anger rises every time you feel pain and feel left out; when you face challenges and fail in life, when you get disappointment, rejected by people you trust and love. Depression can cause your body to accommodate sickness, diseases that Doctors cannot diagnose.

Depression will separate you from your true identity; it can change your character and make you someone that is aggressive and rude. I wrote this book to share my story as a survivor and with a complete new life.

Depression can become an unnoticed friend in your life circle. It is hidden and people will be quick to realise the signs in you and become afraid to associate with you.

Depression wants you to be alone and it will tell you that you are not accepted by the world/ people because you do not see it but your behaviour will tell. Depression will leave an everlasting mark and label even if you have changed, you need to overcome and survived it. You need to fight it…

1

Introduction

Many people have emotional scars caused by their childhood background, is either the scar was caused by their relationship with both parents and the father, or the mother and or it can be anyone you are close to who can affect you emotionally. Your character can also affect you emotionally if it is not accepted by people you associate yourself with.

The environment that you grew in can reject you and it can cause your emotional traumas with emotional gaps unattended, how people relate or how you relate with people can also affects you emotionally.

All that I know and have learnt is that, as an individual, we have emotional gaps that were left unattended and you can grow with them for the rest of your life. This scar will determine your personal relationship with people, either in your love life, your family and your friends or even in the workplace.

Depression is for everyone and it is in all of us if it is not realised and dealt with it at the early stage. Signs of tension, are early wake up call. Sickness related to tension can assist to start looking for signs of depression. We all need to deal with it...

The challenge starts when you begin to engage with someone, commit to each other knowing somewhere deeper, inside of your heart that, there is an emotional scar that you did not deal with and overcome in the past. It is hard to prepare for any disappointment, some warnings are not visible or easy to detect.

Some of the time, it is our ignorance thinking that we are strong enough to handle difficult things on our own. I used to think I am strong internally or my heart is strong until I was hit by depression. It was time for it to trigger. It was time for me to cry and to cry loud to take out the pain; and the pain of my past life…

The solution is, you need someone who you can talk to about these emotional gaps in your life, someone who you will trust and be open to, and someone who will not judge you based on these scars and experienced person you need, the decision lies with you. When we commit to be in a relationship, there is each other's burden that we come along with, thus including emotional gaps of our childhood experience that were not attended.

We both need to be in a positive therapeutic process to each other and support each other as a healing process to our past experiences. If I had to be in a relationship, I need someone who I can be able to confide to, be confident enough to share anything with, receive comfort and not someone who will open my past scars and make it a wound again.

I need someone who I can easily communicate with, be honest with my fears, uncertainties and doubts for our relationship. So it should happen to the same person to. We should build a foundation of trust in any relationship.

Many people cannot maintain any form of relationship. How we relate to each other, it is vital for our daily progress in life. The world is full of broken families, marriages etc.

Depression needs a therapy; it needs support and needs a forgiving heart to heal completely. When you fight depression, you are in the correction, restoration and greener pasture (new life, new beginning process) process. You correct your past and allow God to restore what you have lost in the past; your dignity and value. This experience was my turning point.

You have to get to a process or stage where you focus on the greener pastures; opportunities and success of your life.

You will need to activate a new way, to approach pain in a different matured way, accommodate what is right and positive in your life after depression. There is no pull her/him down syndrome anymore. This is what happened to me.

Any person with Depression can decide to travel or relocate anywhere to do away with the environment that has triggered the depression, believing that things can and or will change. The fact is, you can travel but as long as you are still dealing with the inner person who needs emotional revival to heal completely. This will travel with you…it will be your burden to carry everywhere you go. The reality is, it is not left somewhere there, it is with you.

The challenge can be when you come back from where you went, you will still find what you ran away from, waiting for you to deal with it, you could have faced the reality to the cause of your depression and overcome it, and I believe, that God will always help you to correct any perceptions around your depression status. He did the same to me.

I am still staying in the same environment where my depression triggered, facing the same people who were involved; with courage, boldness, I am succeeding because I am focusing on my purpose, my gift. Remember you were emotionally wounded with emotional trauma and it needs to heal.

The inner man is hurt and needs to heal for the sake of your wellbeing. All that you need is to travel with the objective of getting the therapy as part of your healing process and not to run away from your situation.

That emotional scar in you is part of your reality that will always be there and need you to deal with it tremendously. That is the scar that will always be there to look at, but without pains if you are truly healed.

The same scar will always be a reminder of all the realities that you were faced with in the past, with mistakes, with incidents that are not reversible, but there is no way to change what happened with your situation because it did take place and in the past. This is irreversible but can change and it can transform you to become a better person. The decision lies with you...

You can change how you perceive the status of your depression, from back at what happened to you in the past without pain but with victory because you have overcome the situation or the challenge thereof. Do not avoid any emotional traumas, do not underestimate any sign of hurt, do not regard it as small or big, as long as it causes pain that is not healing, it will wait for the other pains to trigger. This experience can build something that will burst into something big in a long run, with negative decisions and drastic health impact.

The process of your therapy needs healing, forgiveness and peace to whatever that has happened to you in the past. Even yesterday is the past. Hanging on what someone did to you in the past cannot take you to any level of peace.

We are created and born to become strong, with courage to grow as better people. We are created to overcome our challenges with faith and hope to succeed in life. We must live a significant life no matter what. God has never said we will not face challenges. He said, He will be with us through the process of any challenge. Life has a season of transition, to become moved to another level of experience, to measure the stages of our maturity.

He said in His word "I will never leave you nor forsake you, the battle is not yours but mine and I will recompense". He also said in Isaiah 43:18-19 'Remember not the former things, nor consider the things of old. See, I am doing a new thing; now it springs forth, do you not perceive it? I will make a way in the wilderness, rivers in the desert, to give drinks to my chosen people" I am saying these scriptures as my favourite word that has helped me to deal with my past pain and this brought me strength and hope to find the real me, my true nature.

I know that God was with me all the time because I survived the worst and I am still here looking young and beautiful; with His everlasting wisdom and I am focusing on my potential to succeed in life. To leave a legacy, a mark of survivors of life challenges.

2

Who I was.....

I Have been a victim of depression from the early childhood because of my social background, how I grew to where I am now. I was not aware that it will haunt me for the rest of my life until I accepted that I needed a professional help.

My Depression started when I felt anger and bitterness inside of me because I developed an emotional state that would tell me I am left out by the world around me, people that I trusted disappointed me and also rejected by them where I could not have answers for, why me?. One thing that I realised and learnt from this experience is that, people who you trust and or close to can either build or destroy you inside. They can destroy who you are, who you want to become and your natural personality.

All that I know was to revive the inner person, do self-realization and move on with my life. I do trust people, but also to have a room where I would not create any expectations from them but to the one who created me. I had to learn to create a room of disappointment and learn how to manage it.

Finding my purpose was a struggle, but I had to learn to focus on my personal abilities and direct them to where I want to go, what I want and see how to achieve in life. This became the best decision that defeated the status of my Depression.

This was not about people, but about me, how to pull my strength and become a testimony. I had to shape, the new me, I had to tell a story and I had to live and fulfil my purpose without compromising what the world, people perceive about me. I had to allow God to reconstruct and mould me as my potter.

I had to remove all negative words like, "what will people say or think about me". Depression can be your friend and enemy that you need to detach yourself from and for the rest of your life. All that I know is that, I had to take a decision in the midst of professional therapy process and survive it.

The decision was with me to survive it or live with it for the rest of my life. I had to decide if I chose to listen to the negative affirmations that my mind was telling me or to listen and make a conclusion out of the positive affirmations with best outcomes.

People had to diagnose me but I had to correct it, and live a lifecycle where my image and value was restored to my wishes. All that I can do was to visualise greener pastures with courage and faith that I will make it happen and become a successful woman no matter what.

There is an emotional gap that I felt and it continued to grow inside of me, without solutions, because of my social background. Somewhere when I realised that trap that I was in, I would be filled with regrets. The other reason would be the environment that I grew up in, the negative influence of every stage of my growth, the history of my childhood, how my real father left me, my teenage to adult life including family life. The culture of how things were done to and for us.

The Socio-economic lifestyle and background was bad. These became a negative impact in my lifecycle, including the behaviour of people I grew close to, regarded as my relatives and neighbours. The moral values, how they were practiced in the environment that I grew in. The fact is, how I grew, did determine how I lived to date. I had to change; I had to transform to become a better person, who was born innocent before the world can influence her negatively.

This became a battle to fight back, pray without ceasing, and deal personally with all these emotional gaps in order for me to be recognised again, in the world of success. The change of how I live, do things, related with people and especially how I relate with God had to happen.

I had to take a decision either to continue to live the way I grew, or to change that completely. To also change how people think about me in any action of my respond to them, how I feel and how I also approach things, matters most to me.

I had to also, change my attitude and behaviour to what I can face as reality of life. I had to ask God to change me, change my character. I also had to learn to have positive solutions for myself to heal inside and uproot the pain out of my system. I had to learn to do personal introspection before countering to any situation.

There will always be confusion when one is trapped under these kinds of emotional gaps. To take a decision and look for a professional help is a process, either you continue to die inside with what is destroying you for the rest of your life, without any assistance and forget about the purpose of your life or you seek for a therapy.

Psychologist are there trained to facilitate our status of emotions, to help us to become calm and find ways to who we are, they do facilitate the process for us to make a decision to find our strength within. To move out of such situations, but it takes two to tango and the decision lies with you as an individual to move out of this dark pit of depression.

They are not trained to be there for the rest of our lives but can assist, to facilitate and to be guided by our decision, to change and overcome depression. I had to learn that I am the ambassador of my life; I had to make a decision to survive and overcome depression.

I had to learn that there are different seasons in my lifecycle, that there is a season that will favour me and that will not favour me.

To know and understand that all these seasonal changes, can take away my self being or my inner strength. I had to learn that life is not easy but we do struggle, work hard and push further to make it easier. I had to learn that it is not about proving this to the world but evidencing this to me, so to understand my purpose in this world that is full of mysterious challenges. The question to me, every time I would face challenges was "why am I on this earth? I had to learn to make a common decision to survive it with its complicated seasons.

Considering professional assistance and talking or bottling out what was happening in my life survived me. Whether you are a quite person or not, the reality is never in your life say you are fine and strong with something that is troubling you and pretend to be ok. This can trigger in the long run and in a negative manner. The challenge is it can trigger out and can even affect innocent people if they are not aware of the signs of depression. This affected my family and people around me.

Many of us had lost people who loved us, who we were fully depending on, with our emotional gaps. People who we loved so much, not to even think of losing them, because of these emotional gaps that were not attended at the early stage. Communication in many ways can assist you to deal with whatever that is bothering you, as long as the cause of pain inside of you is still there to affect you, it can be a serious wound that needs to be healed.

We all need to find ways to heal, find ways to forgive and find ways to live by being ourselves, teach the world to accept us the way we are and also learn to accept people the ways they are.

One thing that I had to learn when I was writing this book was 'There is no one who is perfect' but we learn through our life experiences to become perfect. God can only perfect us because He created us in a perfect way before we became influenced by the environment that we grew in.

All that we need is to accept each other's weaknesses and learn how to manage each other at all levels of our character as individuals or as a group of people. We need to learn to live or become a acquaintance with each other, know our weaknesses, understand each other, talk about our situations with trust; compromise and support each other because we all need a person who will do the same for us and for our entire lives. This is the reality of life and its consequences.

All that I know is that, the decision lies with an individual, that is take it or leave it, either you become part of each other's life or not because we all need to become comfortable with our attitude or behaviour towards each other instead of pretending to become happy, whereas deep inside our hearts we know we are not about each other and fake our being. This will show out soon with negative effects. It is either possible or not conceivable to related or be with each other.

To pretend to be comfortable with each other when deep inside, we know we are not is dangerous. This can destroy our emotionally, attachment in a physically and psychologically way.

I had to learn that I had to live according to what I want and prefer. I had to know and understand what makes me happy. I had to learn that my happiness comes first and also understand that the happiness of the other person is also a priority to them. I had to learn that when I compromise, each one of us need to fully understand our SWOT analysis (strength, weakness, opportunity and threats of life) and that we all need to analyse them before we become commitment and to live a better life.

Committing to any person is a journey of moving with the person with their shadows and or their burdens including their emotional traumas that were left unattended in his/her past. This is a long term commitment, a lifetime relationship and with all the risk that we all can take. There is no guarantee of how or what life will unfold in the long run when people are committed to each other. In marriage they always use the words, through thick and thin even if it is not broken down, for people to understand the total meaning of these words.

The fact is, we will end up being under each other's shadow for the rest of our lives and this needs team work, to commit to reach both our goals together in the journey of our lives.

It is not easy to manage a relationship or a commitment to any person, from mother/father to children, boyfriend/ girlfriend and husband and wives up to the entire community and the outside world. It is a life journey and some cannot even tolerate each other in the challenges ahead of them, overcome them and enjoy each other in this journey of commitment. There is always a resistance to change or to accept how realities of life work.

The challenge can be, can we understand each other and work things out for better because we do have diverse characters. All that I know is, we dwell much into pain that creates grudges and or personal grudges that lasts forever, than solutions. This is destroying us as individuals and the society. The world is full of anger. We all need to heal.

Family is everywhere, love is natural and always there, it depends on how we embrace the love that we have for each other and find our inner peace within. The question is 'can we compare love with hatred' can you say you love someone and hurt them tomorrow, is it fair enough? This is regarded as betrayal when there is no love and when we are pretending to love one another with our own hidden reasons and this is what the world is. We even forgot that love is kind; love is patient, that it does not hold grudges like it is defined in the word of God. God is love…

When you love something and or someone, you will never destroy them but if there is emotional gaps that where left unattended from the past, you will do the opposite, one can give moral support and become part of the therapeutic process for the healing of the victim of that condition. I had to learn to deal with the past pain, I had to manage my anger and defeat the bitterness that was in me, that was changing the jolly, kind person that I am. I had to find my total happiness with peace I started to prevail and become myself, the person I am today.

The decisions that I took made me realise my gift, the gift that survived me to date. The challenge that I can pose to angry people is that, we do not even realise that we have a gift. We do not even teach other people especially, our youth, to learn to understand their gifts because some of us are angry and trapped with guilt of our past mistakes. We die with our gifts because of the past pain.

The world is becoming destroyed gradually because the Depression had taken over through anger. The respect to each other is gone, we do not value each other, and we do not value our tradition and religion. The value of each other's live depend on our economic status of living, position we acquired, the family background etc. The world is losing its perseverance; people are losing their drive, the energy to lead positively because we are all depressed.

We consider depression when we are diagnosed, without even considering the signs and work on them at the early stage. I use to say I am a strong person, hard worker but I didn't realise that I had a weakness that nearly destroyed my life. That is the pain that was growing inside of me and pretending that I am fine, without considering professional help at the early stage.

I nearly lost my life, my image and my significance. I nearly forgot that I was determined to try new things in life from teenage level as an influential youth leader. My gift was hidden through depression. I am blessed to have realised that, to make a research about it and understand that it started at my childhood life.

These books, are telling a story, my story and this can challenge any person even any leader of any kind of position can go through what I went through, the difference can be what can trigger that depression? We all need to realise our values and cherish every moment that we are given to become what we were created for, before it is too late.

This is where I was able to can share out my fears, and frustrations instead of sharing it with someone who is not professional and also frustrated like me in different ways by writing my books. I had to stop judging myself from my past failures and mistakes. I had to stop hating any person who can take out their frustration to other innocent people instead of dealing with their status of anger.

I had to block accusations, allegations from people who will not even give me solutions in a positive way. I had to deal with the inner me deeply through prayer and meditation. I had to embrace the outside nature of me and allow the world to appreciate and admirer my nature. I had to appreciate myself first, without waiting for compliment from other people.

In the olden days you will be referred to stay with close relatives, uncle, sister or aunt at which, it will be difficult to open up completely and get solutions that you want, to reduce your anger and bitterness. This is what happened to me. I stayed with different relatives from my childhood to my teenage age. It was difficult to find a consistent family figure that I could look up to. I was this confused young person who strived to find her way out to have a meaningful life. My mother was busy working hard to find us a proper home for all of us and it was taking long for her to become approved for a plot of her own.

I remember when I grew up being send to live with different relatives, some did not have kids because it will be a reason that my mother have many kids; I will be send to one area to the other to stay there for a while, whilst my schooling was also disrupted. There was still an emotional gap of why should I not stay with my parents permanently. With many reasons and being with confusion; it was not discussed with me but a decision will be taken and I will pack my things and go to live in a new environment. I saw my elder sister staying with some relatives and she was never happy. This was happening to my other younger sister.

I would see what was not making them happy but I didn't have the authority to question that or come with a better solution. It was also hurting for me to experience that.

In life, do not underestimate how your children feel comfortable at the early age in any place or in the presence of some other people. This can affect them till to their adult stage. You can realize their expression at the age of 2yrs if they are not happy and work on it, to find the truth behind these expressions. As parent try to manage their involvement in any environment that is affecting them and try to be part of their decision as they go along with their growth. Many parents have missed to connect or bond with their children because of not having a proper home for them, some children were taken away by child welfare and this can also affect some of these children emotionally.

Allowing a child to grow knowing that their parent are out there is painful, that their parents cannot afford to take care of them is painful or growing in an environment that is negative, is a disaster. Many of us were influence by the environment that we grew in with negative perceptions and influential activities.

Parents should learn and know that any child who is denied the opportunity to be with their parents is totally wrong.

The child will grow with emotional gaps that are unattended and this can destroy their lives at that early age, to where they will become a husband/wife and or a friend to someone; carrying the past pains or questions that where not answered.

If you are a parent today, work on your past pain and contribute positively to make sure that your children will not experience the same things that you experienced especially when it comes to pain, anger and bitterness; that can affect them at the early age. Your anger can be their anger and that will determine their future.

If I remember well, I was always sent out to help my relatives with domestic work. I was living under my mother's fears of belonging to her relatives. She truly wanted to belong to them and she will do her best without realising the worst out of it. She would even take us there to help them with any request that they will ask her to do. All that I remember now was, my mother grew as an orphan, she needed to be loved, accepted and appreciated and couldn't find her purpose than living under the shadow and the authority of her relatives. Her life was difficult and with us, it became worse.

Finding solution to my emotional gap was not easy; I had to look beyond the past life of my mother's life, how she grew and who she become, when she gave birth to us. That was a painful life experience that I will not ever wish to live or have. The question is did my mother had a choice, at time, no; she did not have the knowledge of how to find her freedom.

All that I know now, is that I do have any choice or can make any decision to fix what she went through by becoming a person stronger than her. She did her best, it was not easy for her but it is easy for me because in the past there was no effective professional assistance. As for us, today, we have countless social welfare programmes and assistance that we can rely on for intervention, as women and as children. There are also the spiritual counsellors to access even through technology, all over the world to can find for therapeutic intervention. There are motivational books, videos etc. that can be easily accessed to assist in our therapy sessions.

I cannot keep on blaming my mother or my parents till I die and or become completely destroyed without living my purpose or finding the gift that I am born with. I cannot continue shifting blames using "if my mother/father didn't do this and that'. I have to live with that as the past and I have to find solutions to live a better life, my life and not their lives.

All that I can do is to tell a story and how I survived. All that I can do is to be thankful that my late mother did her best because I am still here alive. If she could have told me more of how she tried, I will be shocked. They do try and my mother truly tried that is why I survived depression. Her strength, working hard to raise five children as a single mother, is not trying but achieving. Three are married, surviving marital challenges out of her five children.

That is her legacy of survival as a woman of substance. We do not have parental support to date but we are surviving to date. We are parenting each other. We are best friend to each other and that is her inheritance that she left us with, her wish to see us taking care of each other no matter what, through thick and thin, to understand each other's character till death do us apart. To live with faith, love and hope in the mist of difficult life experiences and we are still surviving to date.

She had her own ways of life and she survived it in her own technique. I am writing this book mentioning her because she is my inspiration, she was not perfect, had to learn from her that nobody is perfect but only God can perfect us. Her forgiving heart, love to her relatives has never changed even when she was experiencing their rejection and disappointment.

She will always use forgiveness as a tool, for her to heal. She will smile even if it was hurting but giving us hopes that things will change for better. Her kindness was hiding how people treat her. I used to say I hate her heart when I was witnessing her life experience, how her relatives treated her, that her good heart was attracting pain and wicked people.

I have learnt from her hard working skills that she was doing and trying all her best, to become this perfect person a sister, mother, wife even when the world was rejecting her. She lived her life where her happiness would supress her past pains and experience.

She was a 'mother' and will remain a mother because I am brave to share my story to promote forgiveness and to find our inner peace from our past painful experiences.

I have learnt that I will always have fears of unknown and I will be reminded of my past. All that I remember is, my past is over. I had to close the chapter of my past life. I can tell a story, but it doesn't hurt me anymore. I had to go through what I went through and my family experience for a better life that we have to date.

The blessing that we have is that we are here and are still surviving. I had to learn that some painful experiences of the past cannot be irreversible, but I can only chose to deal with them, find my happiness, peace and move on; to focus in the future and what it holds for me.

This is a process, a process of healing and we do not need to be hard on ourselves when dealing with our past painful experience. We also need to heal and transform to become the positive human beings. Many times I will tell myself I will be strong no matter what but I still have my weakness when I could feel provoked and had to control my emotions. All that I know is that, I will continue to survive, deal with my emotional gaps, attend them and survive every sign of Depression. This will make my late mother proud.

I strongly believe that sharing this story to heal, is what she wanted from me because the outcome of this story is that, I have survived the Depression.

I have overcome its challenges and I am to today someone with high self-esteem. I am special, unique and highly favoured by God. I am an active inspirational sister. I have a huge heart to love and I am always reminded that life is too short, so today I live the best out of it in a positive way. I have a journey to complete, a destination to reach and goals to achieve for better or worse.

There is no way that someone who is not your parent can tolerate all your inabilities and weaknesses like your parents can do; some people can try but it is not easy, it needs a kind heart and a kind character.

They can try for a while but it is not guaranteed as much as it was your parents who should look at your behaviour with all your weakness, life threats and teach you how to manage them, for them to be there for you in all circumstances and experiences of life would be a special gift or blessing that one can cherish for the rest of the entire life.

With my personal experience it was not easy, especially when the relatives had the children of their own, who were in the same age as ours, there will always be discrepancies into our growth and how we were treated and that is what happened to me. This was also creating tension amongst us as children in the same roof, thus creating favouritism and discrimination when there is task allocation in the house.

It was a blessing when we spend the last seventeen years of our lives with my late mother where we realised who she was and our position in her heart. Our new home was a blessing, her own house, her own rules, fair task allocation, warm love and family bonding etc. It was amazing because she told us many stories of her survival. She did experience depression that was not attended but all that I know grace fell upon her life to survive us. She also became born again Christian; in her last 10 years of life and her relationship with GOD, her FAITH, became meaningful to all of us. This last experience with was amazing.

I do believe that there is always a happy ending in every journey of life as long as there is faith and hope. We bonded with her like never before and this I will always keep in my heart. She became our best friend that we would forget her age when she was with us. God gave her and us a time to spend together before she died.

We needed more from her but God's plan was fulfilled. Her mother died without her own house or home for children, my mother did not and strived to get herself a home for us, and we had a home when she died. For us, it was correction, restoration and a grace to greener pasture.

We have corrected many of our emotional gaps, we got a chance, and some people didn't or will not get this kind of chance to achieve something with their parent and we did get this chance, which was a blessing to us and her.

When I look back in the past, I stayed almost in five people's homes, in different areas that I would one day thought that my parents wanted to get rid of me. I did not have guts and power to face and ask them. If I had to complain to my mother, it was either, I am disrespectful or I must hang in there because these people were contributing something in my life, assisting my mother but in return, she had to pay it back by working for them. I was suffering the consequences of my staying in their homes and that this was a favour and in return had to do laundry, ironing, cleaning and cooking at the age of 10 for them and for me to survive. Washing dishes was my everyday task because I hated it until I accepted that it is my duty whether I like it or not, whether their kids helped me or not. This was an obligation. I did it until I started to enjoy it. Today, I hate washing dishes with all my heart.

Today, I am laughing because I do not like to wash dishes and it is my weakness. My family and friends knows that I can do my best to cook the best meal ever but doing dishes is not my favourite activity at all. My family loves my food but they always ask me to minimize messing the kitchen up because I know I won't be washing any dish that I used, it is their responsibility, hope my husband will understand.

All that I am saying is that, it is always fulfilling when we are together as sisters with our children to spend the day at my mother's house and share our past experiences with laughter. For us these experience has sense of humour because it is our past, we survived and overcome the worst of it.

Some environment differs, how we grew and became treated in a bad way, had the most negative impact to our emotional gaps. The early we take a decision to deal with every aspect of our emotions the better; this was my sad story but it will inspire many people who want to overcome their painful life experience too.

When I share my story, many people would ask me, how come did I not die, in the midst of these life experiences because some people are destroyed by only one experience but as for me, for my family, we survived; it will be accidents, life trauma, unemployment, hospital admission through sickness and incident of allegations after the other but we survived with happiness at the end. One of the other best experiences that survived us was singing praise and worshipping songs together with my late mother and one of my aunts until dawn. We had the grace to deal with all these situations with courage. God was there with us.

We would be a full choir, praise and worshiping with my mother in our home, that one day one of the people who were passing by my home knocked at our door, because at that time he thought we were having a church service. This is the best memory that we had with our late mother.

For us as a family, it was a therapy to sing gospel songs and it became her legacy that when we have a sleep over at my mother's place, we will become fulfilled when we sing and pray before we depart to our different homes.

I grew with a low self-esteem personality, even at school I would be this poverty labelled girl who never realised that she had a beautiful eyes and a smile. I was told my eyes were big, my forehead too and everything that I was created with was big that I hated to look at the mirror to admire myself. Today I can admirer myself more than ever. I have taught many people to react towards my positive attitude of enjoy every part of my body and thank God for how I was created.

The other incident was to wear big clothes not of my size including big size for my school shoes and uniform. I will be a joke at school when my peers realised that, that was what my parents would have and they couldn't get a chance to change the size so I was left with everything that is big and this was taking away my self-confidence.

It was hurting and I even hated my toes because the shoe size for my feet. Today I can wear sandals because I do admirer my feet. I had to stop how people see or view how I look and stop how I also see myself.

Looking at my family situation, I would not complain but became excited because at the end, I was wearing something than nothing and it was a privilege. This included my school uniform. Today I have a heart to appreciate out of this experience.

The positive affirmation now is, my self-esteem is back to normal, so it can be yours too, with any experience of your life to become confident. Fight for your confidence at all level; bring out that energy to life, for the sake of your joy and inner peace.

I have learnt not to move around in one circle, create a bad comfort zone; I do not want to become stagnant in life anymore because I grew up with difficulties, shifting blames of what happened to me. All that I know today is that, it was not easy BUT it was worth it. I am here and still alive with a purpose.

All that I know is that I have the potential to do what I believe in and that I am able to do things that always amazes people. It was a process to learn my weakness and strength; but I had to push it and lay a new chapter of my life with personal objectives that needed my focus to achieve them. My song was "no more turning back, no matter what"

My mother used to lock my hair when she visited me where I was staying, but deep inside my heart I knew I will be a joke at school.

I never realised that my forehead, big eyes and skinny body was making me unique and beautiful until I was matured. I still have a beautiful natural hair.

Today when I look at the mirror because of my positive attitude, I see this beautiful creature, very young even more than my peers who used to make a joke out of me. I had to work hard to build my confidence and I did it.

Anger and bitterness can also attracts negative people in your life. You will always be in the company of depressed people and it will be your own choice. I had to learn to choose right people where I would be fulfilled with self-realization of my potential. I always pursue myself to be around people who will inspire me and I inspire them too.

All that we want in life, is wisdom of how we treat each other counts, how we address them according to their position in a positive way without judging them from their weakness. I had to learn to respect any person who I make contact with, young and old and how I relate with them count most; I had to learn to appreciate every little thing that I am given and thank God for it. I had to be able to say thank you, I am sorry, I love you and have a good night or day declarations. This is fulfilling to me, it is part of my purpose.

Through my anger, these words were not necessary, it was like I am doing someone a huge favour to greet or interact with them, I was hurting inside of me, I wanted excuses and there were trust issues.

These words are simple and sweet, but if you are negative and angry with past pain, they are meaningless and hard to say them. There is no respect when you are angry. The worst outcome of everything is where you will always think on your own in a negative way, what people perceive about you, you will always try to justify your character and behaviour to suit how you feel in every action, that you find yourself in.

I had to become matured enough to can listen carefully before I respond towards any perception that is addressed or directed to me. It was not easy but I had to work out my past emotional gaps and fit into the reality of life, to learn that life has ups and downs and that no one is perfect.

I had to accept that my family, my relatives are not perfect, they also have their own life issues that made them to act the way they have behaved, especially when they will mention my mother's hidden secrets when there is family conflicts during their gatherings. It was not fair and embarrassing; it was painful to her and to all of us

It was not easy for her to justify what was said out of context. We will become confused if we should blame her or blame how it was presented and the people who presented it. She was also going through difficulties and felt that some of the things she experienced needed to be kept by her secretly in order to protect us from hurting.

We had to find ways to work out things of her past, deal with them for her healing sake and we did it as friends to her. It meant a lot to her, this created a bond with and a huge trust was created amongst us with her involvement.

My late mother would not like to explain many of her painful experience to us because it was indeed creating hatred to her family and leaving her with emotional scars to attend. She had to work on her heart to forgive who ever in her relative, who did hurt and cause her pain in the past. Forgiveness is a process but we had to work on it as a team with her before she passed away.

All that I know from her mouth with her heart, before she became sick is that, my mother forgave many people who she even mentioned their names from her childhood and this made us to understand forgiveness. We are also proud today because we forgave many people even before they departed from this world. It was not easy but we did not want to live with regrets to date because we have dealt with our pain and has forgiven our past.

My mother's life experiences did affect us but she managed to teach us, to make us deal with our own life issues, to forgive and to also deal with the painful scars of our past life experiences and move on. All that we did through her teachings was that above all; God is our key to heal and a father to guide through the Holy Spirit, a provider to any need, than any other person in this world. He created us, He knows our needs and yes He knows our beginning and our end.

I had to learn to define my mother's character; she was not a talkative person, did not like arguments, she did not like to defend herself but she wanted happiness more than anything when people are gathered, for her, it was a totally celebrations of joy and laughter. That is who we are as individuals and as sisters when we are around people to date. I enjoy making people to laugh to their stomach and in tears. I now know that I also have a sense of humour that was hidden by my past pain but I do not want to be disrespected at all.

This family secret; that will bounce back and forth unexpectedly during family gathering and events, was tiring because it will create conflicts, showing wounds of the past, there was not happy ending. Certain individuals will cause pain to other people during the proceedings, creating grudges and hatred. I had to learn that the devil hates families that are united. As people, family or individuals our pride doesn't promote peace when there is a conflict. One person has to facilitate peace with best solution. Spirit of humanity has to overrule pride. It is not easy to many families out there.

When people have social gathering, it is all about grudges and gauging each other's life progress, competing and or comparing success of one another in a disrespectful approach.

Pride prevails when family gathers for any kind of event. Humanity is lifeless. Families are not assisting or supporting each other anymore, is it no more a norm or a cultural principle.

Families are full of accusations, hatred and shifting blames that never ends with solutions. This is affecting our community and the nation's socio economic development. Our social life is condemned. We do not even know the meaning of love, care and support. We do not want to acknowledge our failures and consider how we can deal with them to find peace out of these failures, manage how we perceive each other and correct how we also value one another. The world will have peace.

I had to learn that evil or negative perceptions leads to disputes when family gathering to celebrate unity and there will be a conflict that will make the gathering end with people hating each other. When they part ways, to their respective homes, the resentment is created between members of such families. In the normal circumstances, these gatherings end up taking away the peace within families and leaving them with grudges, pain and many families cannot avoid or manage these types of disagreements.

These gatherings become a platform where an individual who holds grudges uses, to remind each other of allegations made in the past. At the end these kind of accusation doesn't stop every time when families are in a gathering. The grudges piles and wait for such gatherings to happen.

The question is, why is the past issues or incident; the cause, to limit us from uniting, caring and loving each other or as individuals within the structures of the families. These grudges overlap to the next generation. Family trees are becoming meaningless and fading away. Family gatherings are limited or they are failing completely because of anger and hatred. There is always an excuse or apologies to attend such gathering to those who are affected; because other people do not want to meet, see or speak with any individual who has caused conflicts in the past. WHAT DOES GOD SAY, IN THIS REGARD, and FORGIVENES is the key to solve conflicts.

A dysfunctional family can create and or give birth to the lost, confused generations; this is killing the world if the solutions are not attended at home level, where the principles of love should begin; with traditional morals and values, we need to teach and practice this culture to every child born in a respectable family that, family is a blessing.

Our parents were blaming each other for their weaknesses and past mistakes; we are also doing the same, hence it will also overlaps to our children to the generations after generations. It is a chain of angry nation focusing on negative activities without direction to success and economic upliftment.

The challenges that I am stating here says to us 'can we heal?', Can we coach and mentor the generation that will not be depressed like us? Can we find ways to heal; can we all know and find out who we are, what we want and where we are going? Can we find out what makes us happy or unhappy and communicate about it and support each other? Can we do self-introspection? And practice the same principles that we develop and put actions on them like when we do strategic sessions; review our dreams, our goals for the success of families and our companies, organizations that we serve.

We need to use this approach to our disadvantage in our homes, as families to mend what we have lost in the past. We are losing the meaning of the "Family" Why can't we turn the same corporate strategic approach into our personal strategy and review our dreams with SWOT analysis in order to achieve them with courage? (Strength, Weakness, Opportunities and Threats) to improve our lives for better; so that what we practice in the corporate environment is done everywhere we are and or go. We can own this approach anywhere and anytime.

This can be our culture and we can change on how we perceive things or how we grew to manage our families for a better life with bright future. There is a huge need for us to build our communities in a different unique way; this can spread to the entire world with love, peace and unity. To build a free depressed Nation.

There is no need of becoming happy in the working environment and become miserable and frustrated when you are in your home and or the other way round. Depression can steal you time, energy, happiness and your life; by being miserable for the rest of your life. Everything that doesn't work in your life and how you engage with people can depress if you raise your expectation that are not fulfilled, this includes rejection and disappointment. You can buy many material staff, clothes, furniture etc. trying to fulfil the gap of your depressive life. These kind of material cannot take away your depressed life, you need to face it and deal with it and let your inner peace fulfils you…

There are emotional gaps that are unattended and either in one of these areas, either at work or at home. You will suffer the consequences of your emotional gaps. Rather deal with the inner person so that your personal objectives can be in line with your work and company's objectives. There should be a compliment of the two to live a complete happy life.

We are depressed season after season, and we need to acknowledge the signs when we see them instead of ignoring them, deal with the first stage of depression before things can get out of control.

Living a life of being in denial and faking who you are before what you can become, can be a danger to who you become in the long term, when you supress the emotions that are deep inside of you and that are taking your happiness away and or your true identity.

Crying and coughing out what is bothering you are a huge therapy. Pray and find someone who you can lean on to share your fears and pain. There are good people out there who are created and called to listen and advice when you are in pain. The biggest therapy is to laugh and even to smile from the heart.

We are not the same with characters, status and personalities; but we need to work on the signs of Depression before it can be diagnosed to a high stage where you can become critical and end up in the hospital. Depression can change your status of life, and your health. It can create a negative perception towards every behaviour or attitude that you can perform towards other people. It can destroy your image; it takes energy to can convince people that you are no more depressed, it is not easy. It is not easy to remove the stigma of depression.

You will be addicted to something that is abnormal and you can overdo anything that comes your way; you do not need to be corrected, you are always right when you are depressed, you can argue and manipulate any situation.

If you find yourself giving excuses of doing certain things in a wrong way, you think you are not favoured and but you not fulfilled inside. You need to take note of that behaviour and do a review on it, your response to anything including how you respond to any comments in a negative approach can also give signs of your unusual angry behaviour.

That is a way of trying to fill in the gap of your emotions from far in the past to date and also quoting negative words or statement than positive ones around any conversation or when you engage with people around you. Listening becomes a threat to choose what you want to hear and react negatively toward any act. This is difficult to control when people are depressed because they always have their own agenda to fulfil their feelings, when they are hurt and angry.

Some people have died without getting the explanation and or given explanation of why they have suffered in the past.

All that I know is the history is stored in the back of our minds and we become reminded of our past pain. We tend to focus on the pain than the healing process of our soul, spirit and body. There is a lot of negative affirmations than confessing and or declaring positive affirmations to show that we have moved on from our past. I had to learn to block the negative thoughts and declare positive words over my life.

I always tell people to watch what they confess with their mouth as the word of God says "Power of the tongue" is very dangerous, meaning you can be what you have said with your mouth. The challenge that I have was to train my mind to work on the solutions of all my emotional gaps that were left unattended from my childhood. I had to choose to be in denial of having depression or to accept and deal with the condition that I was in. it was not easy.

My teenage life was a mess and I was staying in boarding house when I was in high school. I had to convince my parent to work hard for my school fees by performing beyond their expectations, because, my aim was to avoid to stay with relatives. I do honour my late stepfather for working out my boarding fees with my late mother. Apart from all their weaknesses and emotional gaps that affected them, they did try their best and I was admitted to complete my standard 9 and my matric with flying colours. I worked hard to achieve good result in my studies.

I had to learn and know that there is no one who is perfect; but to also take note that emotional gaps that are not addressed with right decision can destroy you emotionally and psychologically; there is a stage where you can find yourself not having a direction to reach out to your goals because of your depressed life. We are created and destined to succeed in life, but our emotional gaps can bring failures and fears that can make us to remain in one area of life with frustrations and misery. Miserable life attracts rejection and disappointments.

The other challenging social issue was, when I completed my matric. My peers had already planned with their parents for their university admission and college but I was not able to comment my plan; because my parents could not afford financially and the option was to go and look for a job. I became more frustrated.

Depression can destroy you, or you can become strong after dealing with its stages. I had to tell depression that I am not a friend to it, I will not live under its shadows, and that I do not belong to its principles. I had to build my own personal principles and values that I am a strong, beautiful, unique, special, wonderfully made human being; and highly favoured under grace. The more I told myself and confirm these positive affirmations, the more the signs of depression stated to disappear and that is how I found my total internal peace and strength.

I use to hide in my house, I didn't want to make contact or socialise with other people, because I was hurting and angry; there were still emotional gap inside of me. I was afraid that people would ask me many questions about my life progress, what I am currently doing and my future intentions. The best way was to stay indoors without attending social activities. The best outcome of this was, I was able to write a book, I was fighting my emotions and finding myself. I was also in a closet; I call the upper room with God to find myself.

I had to build my spiritual life and this strengthened my relationship with God than ever. I was with God and not alone. I had to pull myself up and see the world in different way, identifying business opportunities. That is how I was able to realise my purpose, that I am still needed in this life.

I had to pursue what I am capable of. That is my potential to speak, to share and to inspire people. I completed my Diploma, registered a business, went out and became a motivational speaker. Sharing experience with testimonies, made me to write more books and I am currently recognised as an author. I had to move on with my life.

I was sharing to someone that I would stand in the middle of my house and scream loud; asking God to come and take me because I was giving up my life and didn't know my purpose. I believed that He has taken my strength, by taking my mother away from me, because I was still in the depression stage when my mother passed away. It was quite and I needed Him to give me the answer, the answer that I only needed was to see my breath stopping.

I was afraid of taking my life because I knew that if I commit suicide, I will not enter heaven and that was a scary part for me. I wanted and wished that God should do it on my behalf as the holder of my spirit. It became quiet, and nothing happened to date.

All that I wanted was for God to take my life like He did with my mother. After going through the process of forgiving and self-realization, I started to enjoy life. One of my sisters reminded me after I have gained back my strength that I once told God I have allowed Him to come and take me away from this earth.

I kept silent for a while, I kneel down to ask for forgiveness and I asked Him not to take my life because I could now see the light. Life was full of fun and I was telling my story as an overcomer. I did ask Him more years to live.

I was experiencing pain, hurting because of the environmental perceptions that were indirect and directed to me that I wanted to hide and be rude to respond, it was bad for my emotional situation. Rumours were destroying my strength. I was also destroying myself because I was entertaining what people think about me. I had to learn to control my emotions and believe in myself more than what people say about me. I wanted to know every day how people perceive me and what I went through in the past. There was this anxiety to know and this was destroying my value too.

I had to revert back and stand firm in what I say, hear and see. I had to draw the line and remove people who bring news that will break and hurt me. I had to take a decision, listen to the news that builds me and be in a company of good and positive people. I started to surround myself with people who are inspirational and who would share my positive quotes to motivate individuals in one of the social media.

I did go to college and it did not work for me, my mind was always back at home thinking about my mother and sisters, asking myself what will happen to them in the midst of a violent father.

I was scared for them when I was living far from home. My college educational background was a mess because my mind was full of negative issues, fears and this was creating a low self-esteem. My parents tried to take me to college and financially they couldn't afford the college fees. One member of our relatives commits that they will assist her to pay my college fees and the promise was not fulfilled.

I was disappointed. I felt that people were failing me, to achieve in life. I was confused. I did work for them with that expectation.

This also destroyed me emotionally because I was left with one year- six months to complete my studies. I had to drop out of college and I was looking for a job. I couldn't find any kind of job because I was negative and angry. My friends tried to connect me and I lost many job opportunities because of my character.

I was confused, I was angry. My family had a pattern of silent, we had fears, we were angry, we would feel guilty and we would live a shameless life. That is how we grew and how my late mother grew.

I had to come back home where I volunteered and this was my first breakthrough and my commitment, the best experience ever, I call it my breakthrough.

I started to volunteer and worked with young people and I also became their leader. I felt my purpose as young as I was, but the emotional gap was still there hidden by my hard work in youth programmes.

This became a huge success that created me a full time job. That is where my passion for youth started. Working with young people became a career and a passion in my nation. This passion will always…always be in my heart to play an important role in our youth.

I did not have qualifications by then, but my volunteering work with patriotic spirit created me a permanent job, in my community. This opportunity created my self-esteem and it was my journey that was unfolding whilst I did not know that there are still challenges ahead of me. This was a chance and a blessing to become recognised for my hard work.

My peers, who I went to high schools with, went to college, university and completed their studies whilst I was home and working hard to create myself a job opportunity and I did it. The positive part of dealing with my emotional gaps was to create this job opportunity for myself through voluntarism with the love of youth and community development work. I initiated youth programmes in community development work and my career was restored.

Deep inside my heart I knew how I felt, my fears and frustrations. I had no exciting news of success to share with my friends. I had to minimize my social lifestyle; interaction with many friends that I went to school with to avoid many questions regarding what I was currently doing. When they come back home from universities, I would hide until they go back because of my low self-esteem.

I had to do away with many friends and became friends with my sisters. As for my sisters, we had been there to support each other through our family experience. It became a bond ever between us; and they knew I had unpredictable behaviour because of my depression and how it triggered looking at my past experience. I have tried to have friends but it never worked because I had many challenges in my life that demanded my attention including my family.

The anger that arose from me was to live a better life, to be respected by people whether I come or grew from a poor background. I needed to be valued by people for who I was and I am today; not where I come from with my painful experience. All that I needed was to be seen in a positive way. I would share my childhood experience which to some people it will make them to reject me or to have shame around them.

During my depression status, the words that came into my mind was, to prove to the world that I can make it, and would always ask my family to strive for a better life.

One thing that I now know is, it takes courage to share a story, for me, this is my best therapy ever. One thing that I realised in the process was, I do not have to prove to anyone but to prove it to myself that I am capable and have the potential to live a successful life. I had to tell myself that either I make a choice to live a better life, become successful and know my position wherever I am and to fulfil my purpose; or to allow the world to see me as shameless as I would accept.

I had to learn that I come first. I had to learn that I have to teach people to respect me, and to teach them how they should treat me. I knew that no one can change me and that I have weakness that needs someone to understand but I also need to manage my reactions towards any situation.

I had to lead people, to honour and identify me as the best human being in their lifecycle, in anything that I say or do. Remember there is a negative perception when you are diagnosed with depression. Some people relate it with mental illness and whatever that you say, their reaction or your response to their approach, can misinterpret what you say to them; it can be you are still behaving like a depressed person.

I had to be careful of what I say or do. How I say it and when to respond to any of the questions asked when I am engaged in a conversation.

I had to train my mind to listen before responding to any provoking statements and even when I address people. When I wrote this book, I was emotionally torn apart that when I read it for the second time, I had to change some contents that where disturbing but showing how I felt by then.

Every year, there was an emotional gap created and was not fulfilled in a positive way but to live with the fear of unknown, rejection, disappointment and frustrations for a long time can damage you. The question that will come into my mind was "do I really belong in this world, can I someday fit into this world's socio-economical activities and benefit, apart from being spiritually active and becoming successful like other normal people?

The other emotional gap was, I never knew who my father was, my mother had courage to tell me who he is but she kept on protecting me to have a bond with him. I tried to have a bond with him but there has been some doubts that are not coming together to say he is truly my father. He has never made any effort to look for me or get to know me, why I do not know. I am not even sure if he is really my father.

My mother told me he never wanted to see me, why I do not know. All that I know is, I had my stepfather in my life. I have accepted this situation and I have found my inner peace in it and I had to move on with my life knowing that I do not have a father.

This is a complicated story where I do not know where the truth lies and to remain where it is. My mother is late and I cannot pursue or know where to start with this situation. It did cripple my emotions and I had to forgive and move on with my life. This was also an emotional gap that was left unattended……

Staying unemployed at home, waiting for an opportunity, also affected me and I will always feel tired without hope. I had to learn that things happen for a reason, that God cannot give you a problem that you cannot handle; and also that there is always hope in every season of difficulties. All that I would encourage myself with was, it is not late for me to try many new things. I am still young and with potential. I had to deal with my fears and also erase the fears that my family had when I was diagnosed with depression.

Depression can make you hate people from any little mistake that you feel they are doing as long as you feel uncomfortable with what they do towards you. I had to experience lot of anxiety and praying about failures and for whomever who did caused me pain in the past. When they fall or fail in the journey of their life, it will be victory for me and this was a bad wish. I had to change my negative perception around all the people who I used to wish that bad things should happen to them if they caused me pain, instead,

I would pray for them to date; I have continued to pray instead of saying a curse. It didn't matter who did what to me but just to forgive and move on. I had my own negative perceptions but now I have a new life.

The way my dignity was torn into pieces, It was difficult to value myself too; even our former neighbours would make a joke out of my unemployment situation; that it persisted to a point where one day we had a quarrel with them together with our mother because they confronted me and attempted to beat me up, I was scared to fight but luckily, my younger sister was there to intervene aggressively so.

I do not know how to fight, so she became my rescue and I gained the strength to fight back and defend myself. Try me where there are stones, or anything that I can throw you with, and then you are in trouble. This was also bad because of wrong accusations. This was also depressing.

Physical contact is not my game of fighting any person but once my younger sister is involved; I will definitely join her to beat the person up. I was happy when we left the old home where my stepfather lived, to stay in a new home that we fought for; it became a happy home to date.

I remember one incident when I went to look for a job, came back tired and these neighbours would laugh at me saying negative perceptions around the disapproval of my job search. This would hit me with a terrible back pain, I felt dizzy and thought I was going to faint to death when their laughter hits me. The veil of rejection and disappointment was covering my life everywhere I go. I was denied to become me, my nature.

The other bad treatment was when my laundry was hanging in the washing line. They would laugh at my clothes based on how they took the shape of my curved legs; because I was this skinny, shameless girl with low self-esteem.

Everywhere I go and or try to relate with people, my confidence was taken away. This woman was even older than me and my elder sister. She attacked me physical with wrong complaints and offense. She was stating negative comments with insults that would also leave me emotionally torn apart. This was also tearing away my self-respect.

I was afraid to attend social activities, because some people were brave enough to can approach me in a negative way and ask me personal questions that will disturb my self-confidence. If you are negative, you will always concentration on how people will approach you. You do not have the wisdom on how to control their mind-set towards the status of your life. It normally comes out unexpectedly.

If there were rumours behind their questions, there will always be someone who will want to confirm if, it is true perception that I had depression. Some questions would be around my marital status, if I will have children of my own or not and when? I got used to these questions and it was well to know that there is a concern that I do not have to justify but to accept who I am because I know what I want and what I have planned to achieve.

The positive affirmation would be at the right time and God time is the best. This statement will always be my response and it has saved me. As an individual and as a family, we had something unique and special that we were not aware of.

People would see it, the dignity, the value was inside hidden by how we painfully grew; how we were treated badly by some people that we trusted and believed that we are part of them.

There was still something unique and bigger that was inside of me that needed revival. One of the greatest thing was I had wisdom of its kind, God given, where I would give a solution to any problem when I am approached by someone with challenges. This was natural, it just appears that people would approach me for advices and I would respond positively to their expectations; this was unique for me and it promoted my confidence. I would be fulfilled to make this kind of positive impact in someone's life that needed my opinion. I am still doing it, I am consulted even after every motivational tours.

I could have qualified as a Social Worker or Psychologist but due to my family financial struggle. I did not get the opportunity to go to university to accomplish my wish. The positive part is, the potential was still inside of me. The question now is, what can I do with it? There is a demand from many people, requesting one on one session with me for counselling.

I have been motivated and planning to study psychology to embrace my gift and my calling. I want to pursue all my dreams without blaming someone and or by giving an excuse that; if my parent didn't take me to university, I could have been this and became successful.

I had to consider that whether I could have qualified as a Social Worker or Psychologist, I still have the opportunity to go to university; I am still young and alive.

I still have a purpose to live and a chance to encourage myself and find ways to become a better person. Giving excuse and or blaming people can make you to get stacked with anger and bitterness for the rest of your life. You will not see any other opportunities around you, good people too, who can even lead you to where you less expected, your destiny.

I had to learn to try many new things to find my potential, search my interests and look for opportunities with positive approach. I survived along the way of my emotional gaps that were unattended and I am here with courage to embrace what I have and what I can have in the future.

This is a process to consider effectively; because there is a mountain of incidents that has caused me pain as I grow and there are still challenges ahead of me waiting for me to face them; I will with boldness. There are five areas of life that I had to look at during my painful seasons; that are Health, Marital status, Education, Career, Finances, Business and Family where an emotional gap is created and can trigger into depression at the later stage from each of these aspects of life. These areas are part of our socio-economical lifecycle. They create a lifestyle for us in a positive or negative way.

Each of this area, there is challenges; people of different character and status, are involved positively and negatively in these areas of life. One can be affected emotionally when there are failures and mistakes in their lifecycle. The question that came into my mind after realising these areas was, how will I manage these areas? to overcome the challenges within them and survive life changes? It is difficult; it needs God's strength to overcome any challenge coming from these areas. It was not easy for me but I FOUGHT.

We need energy; we need sober, calm mind to fight against depression. We need wisdom and discernment to overcome negative atmosphere. These areas needs good, positive company of people who will give you support and hope when things are tough within each of these areas. These areas needs the best decisions and good healthy choices, that will make you see life with new seasons, and that we are always given a second chance to start a new chapters of our lives after every trial of challenges.

I had to learn that I need people who adores and respect me. I also needed people who will challenge me with constructive criticism. This attitude needs someone who will have courage to risk and learn new positive things that will build his or her character. It sets new personal goals with principles. You have to showcase changes to your character and that there is indeed a new direction of your life worth to live, in a positive way.

My experience was a wakeup call to deal with whatever disapproval or rejection, and accepting to fight for my inner peace, for my positive personal revival and lifetime goal oriented benefits. I took a decision, to do introspection in a positive way instead of giving up easily. I had to learn to fight and attend every attack of my emotions.

We do need good and bad people in our lives for us to transform for better, and or for them to change in life. This is the reality and facts of life; it is a cycle of life with pruning seasons.

The question can be, can you manage the negative waves, even if people are provoking your feelings? Can you have self-control and make peace in your every situation that tempers with your emotions? Can you be strong enough to handle the pressure of not allowing negative people to put you where they want you to be; even if you do not want to, but make peace out of any situation that you find yourself into. It can be deliberate. I had to learn that and make peace out of every challenge that I came across.

This can complete our life in a different, positive way; where people less expected because they can provoke you based on your character or behaviour to judge you. This can also become a plot with agendas, to push you towards where they want you to be by provoking you. This can be intentional to prove their point that you are this kind of a depressed person; who they perceived.

You can make them to achieve what they have said about who you are. Just be careful to who is provoking you to any level and in any environment. I had this experience and it was hurting because it was related to my depression. I believe I have survived and overcome it and so are you. You can survive even if we have different experiences, the pain inside must go away and we must fight to live our purpose.

If you are provoked and you act and respond negatively, they will say "didn't we tell you that she is like this" I do not want the stage where I allow negative people to rule over my life, control me and to also remind me of my imperfections. I had to hate the word former, because I cannot change it, I cannot reverse my blunders but I can learn from them and move on with a better life. God gave me a second chance to live my life to the fullest and to only look up to Him as depression was my turning point.

I had to build a positive attitude to address my historical situations with self-assurance; when people are trying to make a destructive opinion to pull me down. I had to make a joke out of any undesirable statement with confidence to teach them that I have changed. I am a new person and I am moving forward with my life.

You need to showcase your abilities, that you have closed the past chapter of insignificant staff. It is also, when you meet or see people that have caused you pain and you do not feel any discomfort but peace inside of you.

There is peace inside of you whether their names are mentioned; there is still peace and a smile in your face to show that you have forgiven them. That is what happened to me every time I hear the names of the people who triggered my pain in the past; I would be filled with peace, instead of becoming emotional and angry. This was a sign to show that I have forgiven them and that I am rehabilitated completely, because in the previously, it will definitely be offended.

I used to have the pain in my heart every time I make contact with them and or overhears their names mentioned in every conversation that I would engage myself in; and with people who also knows them, my face would change. I would also have a frowny face to express how I felt when hearing their names mentioned. One that I knew in my heart was, I will always make contact with them because some of them work and some stays in the same environment that I live in, or that my family stays in.

The other sign that I had was; I would not justify myself when I am corrected from any fault that I do in my new life; but to find solution to bring peace to the situation. To say I am sorry with facts, would be my positive affirmation and respond with humble approach; even if I knew I was not wrong, the word harmony would be in my inner man all the time when there a conflict or a dispute is created.

I had to learn not to justify myself but to believe in correcting effects with silent manner; this has made me realised my humanity with a smile.

I would be silent; my angel will tell me to be quiet when there are allegations or accusations. You cannot change the past, but you can change the person you are, by pursuing your dreams with courage.

My believe system was that many things will be corrected in many ways by avoiding negative utterances; when there is a need, I need to respond with tact in a positive way, truly there has been many corrections that some occurred without responding to any attack from a negative person.

Sometimes we need to be soundless when we are attacked or provoked in negative manner and to allow peace to rule over our emotions; and to also allow God to fight our own battles. The reward is the peace that you feel inside of you and the happiness that you experience in the long journey of your healing.

With my personal challenges I had to encourage myself with scriptures, this is my special quote in the bible, the book of 2Timothy 1:7 For God has not given us the spirit of fear, doubt but of love, boldness and sound mind" This has taught me to fight every fear that I could encounter when approach by negative people. I will utter this verse every time I am faced with challenges; that I need to be wise and bold when I am in a negative environment and company of people who are with negative sensations.

I use to entertain the label of shame and it followed me everywhere I go; because I was depressed and there was still emotional gap not attended. Even if you can move to another level of success, people who knew how you grew will still treat you with what they know and also see, your behaviour counts to every move that you make. It will be a process to teach them to remove the label of your shameless life. You are still what you are to them and this has to change.

I had to learn to accept that every person has their own opinion and perception when they look at how you live or behave. It is their own cause to decide how they value or think of you. You also need to decide how you accept how they respond towards your actions.

I have to make a decision to do away with depression signs, deal with my anger, hatred and bitterness specifically, towards my past painful experience. I had to close the past chapter because I did not want to hide any more from the reality of this world, rather deal with what is happening in, with my life.

I had to move on and start teaching people how they should perceive me, now to the future. It is not easy to remove the negative perception of any stage of depression but we should not give up but fight against every stage of depression. It takes courage to fight for your value and dignity. I had to train my mind-set and start to believe that I have an authority over my life; I am the executive of life.

I had to minimize to become scared of being in the public and teach people how to treat me in a positive way and deal away with their questions, and their approach. I felt uncomfortable when they are around me that I told myself that I do not owe anyone anything regarding my progress in life.

People ask what they want to hear, they get the response but they will never do anything about it and or get satisfied. They can still need to hear what they expect to hear and your response towards their actions.

I had to train myself to become comfortable anywhere I want to be without fears. You cannot measure my strength towards mine but you can learn to gain your strength through my experience. I can also prepare myself to learn from the same from the people who have inspired me.

I was asked by someone the other day, what I am currently doing for a living and with the hope of being recognised, I responded positively, with excitement that I am currently unemployed, thinking that this individuals who would do something to refer me to employment opportunities and nothing happened.

This taught me to regain my confidence. I had to accept and be open about my status of depression, so to deal with it and teach other people and or victims of depression that we are born perfect and are influence by the environment that we grew in, with bad experience; we become something that can make us act differently.

That is why we need to change and realise our perfect creation. We need to transform from any status of health challenges and overcome every situation that we find we find ourselves in. In every platform where I speak in the public, I would talk about my experience of being the victim of depression and how I became an overcomer to this depression.

I had to learn to avoid what people perceive about my status of depression, accept that I had it and that people do know what I feel inside and what made me to have a negative impact in my life, my career and my love life. I knew deep inside me, that I had to deal with it, fight it and get myself on track to what I believe in. I had to do away with what people think about me.

I had to be honest that I owe it to myself. To fix my life and never to expert that someone would come and fix it on my behalf. You will never meet the expectations of all people who you relate with; meet, work or you are committed to. People have their own decisions and choices to their current lifestyle and how they want their lives to be like.

Either you chose negative friends who will destroy you gradually or positive company that will complete the healing of your emotional status or scars. You need people who will support you through your healing process and not to make it worse. I was fortunate my family was there fulltime to support me and some of my family friends who gave.

I have experience to be alone in almost two years. I have experienced loneliness and had to allow fears and doubts to conquer my inner strength; I would feel trapped and became a topic again and again about my status and I would allow this to over shadow who I am and where I am supposed to go. I was not attending their social events, whether I was there joining them or not, I will still be a concern.

The questions will always be how much do I owe to them to share my progressive life or the current status of my family life? I had to say no, to many of perceptions that were related to my status. I had to believe that I am not going back to my emotional gaps in the step of my healing process. This was the cost of living with depression, what it can do to you, and what you can do about it is very important. The decision to overcome it lies with you.

You are not doing anybody favour to forgive but you are healing because if you are not forgiving, your mind will be contaminated with negative thoughts; you will always wish the worst to happen to the lives of those who made you a victim to depression.

You only think of revenging. You wish to find ways to know what is happening in their personal lives, that will indicates that they are suffering and you become happy when things are not going well in their lives.

This is hatred, this is the negative energy that you use towards people who have caused you pain. There is no room to forgive. Forgiveness has to be a decision that you personally take when you do away with pain and release yourself from people who have caused you the pain. If the people who have hurt you face challenges, you feel that your wishes have come true and that they are punished. This is not right at all.

You are tortured with a life of cursing people who have caused you pain. You are stacked into their failures because you have to get the updates now and then on how they live their lives. When you meet them, you want to see mistakes in their physical appearance. You are in your own world full of negative perceptions and bad wishes. I had to forgive them; I had to pray for them.

After realising that I am spiritually matured, it was when I heard myself praying and calling the names of people who have hurt me, for God to bless them as the lost souls and that God should forgive them. I had to believe that I am not fighting flesh and blood but principalities of darkness and evil spirit behind them; that is pursuing them to become angry with everything and everyone they relate or work with; because of their own personal emotional gaps that were not attended from their childhood.

I got sick in many occasions, every year I will be admitted in the hospital or my family member. It is scary but there will always be perceptions from people who are close to me; where

I will hear rumours of the negative diagnoses that are not even in my sick note from my Doctor.

I had to learn a lot from rumours, gossips and deal with how I accept and address them. It is funny that people who you trust and are who you are close to, are the ones who spread the status of your health easily and the question to me was, how can I justify myself from this allegations if it is already spread? Do I have the energy to go into details from person to person who have heard what was going on in my life and explain; what was the cause of my sickness?

Whether I can explain it, they would still, it was not going to work out to become positive or believe what I have to tell them, already they had convinced conclusion of my status and I would make no sense of requesting assistance too. It was hurting because sometimes the Doctors would not trace the cause of my sickness but to align it with tension and stress symptoms. I was indeed in a dark world and trying to show people that I have a light in me and my future is bright too.

It was the sign of depression and my mind was full of negative beliefs. I had many grudges because of gossips, rumours. When I am alone the negative self-talk will make me more angry when I recall or being reminded of what had hurt me. I would select bad memories more than good memories; which I had in the past and not to consider any happy event which I had because I was angry.

The world of Depression doesn't give you a chance to appreciate, love and care. You will struggle to do anything positive including to utter positive words like I love you, thank you and I am sorry.

You will feel that you are not obliged to say these sweet words that humble us; you will feel like you are doing someone a favour to say this generous of words. Even when I greet people with a smile, I will draw the energy to generate the smile. I did not even know that I had a beautiful attracting smile until I was healed; because you do not want to lose your smile to them who have caused you pain, I could not pretend to be happy and smile when I knew my heart was aching with pain.

This behaviour will make people to realize that I do like or want to associate with them and it didn't bother me at all. I would make them perceive that I am this reserved, quiet person, but again negatively I would still complain when I am also not appreciated or recognised. I did not know what I wanted that could fulfil my empty heart filled with misery.

I had to learn to teach people that, they should treat me with respect and I had to earn it by also showing them the respect. It had to start with me; I had to be positive towards me first, in many ways where I became a priority to make myself happy. I had to find peace in the midst of criticism and pain. I had to train myself to become positive by all means and respond positively towards any question or comments. When I greet people with a smile I felt peace.

My smile was my biggest sign of peace. When I say I am sorry, I will still feel peace, when I say I am thankful, I will feel the same peace; and saying I love you will fulfil me internally and my smile would prevail and conquer my frowning face.

I also practiced these words to many people who I met and their reaction will tell that we all need to be told and share these kind words to each other without favour or obligations. This should be natural, my positive affirmations released my heart and my beauty started to reflect to get many compliments of being young against my age. These kind words were also giving me freedom to myself being, my nature of a loving person.

The world's view and perceptions can rule your life and you will always feel weak when you hear the hearsays that implicate you; because confronting people is also a waste of time, it can turn your dignity away with a negative label of disrespectful person.

One thing that I know is, people have hurt me in the past and most of them I did not do anything to hurt them and I had to deal with it to my peace. I was having emotional scars, these scars attracted bad people who made negative impact in my life. This has to stop for good by creating a courageous attitude towards everything.

All that I had to learn was; as people of God, we have choices to make and a better life to live with or without other people's influence, we can decide to be involved in bad actions or chose not to get involved.

Some of us, we will lose many opportunities in the journey of our lives because of our choices; we can also gain more opportunities if we make good choices; meet other new people who will make sense in our achievable goals. We will lose friends and gain other friends, we will mourn for our lost family members and still continue to live, face challenges, fail, succeed etc. but we will still need to live a healthier life.

We need to avoid the people who are negative in our life, the decision lies with you if you need a progressive life. I do not want to live a life where I am under the negative shadow that is created for me to suffer for the rest of my life and this will continue to cause pain if we allow it.

This will also attract bad people who will pull you down and at the end you will encounter fear when you have to try new things. You will be scared to approach people who can even help you towards achieving your set goals. I had to remove myself from this kind of negative energy and shadowed myself with positive affirmations. I am here living with a purpose and God's purpose.

I had to learn that I was born with the strength before the world can influence my negative life; I knew deep inside that

I was hurt but the pain should not persevere for a long time. I was born with a purpose and I need to embrace it.

My social background and the environment that I grew in with people I grew with, affected my life in a negative way, not all of them but some and I had to face the reality that came out of this experience. I was only concentrating and was focusing in to those who continued to hurt me not realising that I was opening a door for depression.

All that I know is that Depression is there and we have to fight it no matter what. When I look back to this kind of life, I was trapped in a cage of emotions, in Afrikaans language we say "Jy is agter trallies' and my family was trapped too causing damage to know and understand who we are, how to fit in this world. I was not coming with a better solution as a strong bone in the family, as a leader in my mother's house but making things worse. I felt accountable for all our failure and felt responsible to correct it.

The worst thing was when my family couldn't be tough enough to stand on my side, to justify what they know about my situations, it was not easy for them to protect me from all these world views.

I have always given them the impression that I was this strong sister, the strong bone in the family, the bread winner, the survivor and the hard worker but the survivor fell down, I was torn apart because the lighting of Depression stroked me down that I forgot my name. The truth is; my life was falling apart. I was seeing myself going down into a dark pit where no one was able to pick me out of it. I could only see the dark. I had to fight my emotions to see the light in my life.

Tears that drained my energy became a solution to my depression status. I couldn't control myself from crying every day; sleeping for a while would help temporarily. I fell, lost my love life, my job, my mother who was the strength for me to survive many challenges in my life; I lost this in the same year. It was a dark life experience and my downfall. It was not easy but today, it was worth it, I feel blessed and highly favoured by God.

I will know that the rumours will become a true reflection to the perceivers than the real truth if I remain in the dark pit. The question would be "Do I really have the energy to go door to door and correct what was said or perceive about my situation? The answer is NO, it is well, it was my season and it will come to pass that the perceivers will forget that I was once a topic of the world of their entertainment full of undesirable perceptions.

If people are concern about your life and or the situations that you are experiencing, some people will not question but become anxious to support and assist me; but some people will complete my story in a negative way, and this was very wrong. There will always be volunteers who will assist, support me in silent. They become part of me, to understand my experiences with prayers. The answer for them, about my situation will appear automatically because they were part of my life with prayers.

They will always defend me, because they knew me and know what I was going through. They would give me hope with a smile.

I consider them as my angels and I respect them to date. These are the kind of people who will give you a chance and or an opportunity to draw you energy back. They will believe in you and show it by many ways. Pray to have them in your life.

They always reminded me of my heart to God. My family did the same by accepting to build a strong relationship with we are surviving to date. I remember this kind, loving and caring lady pastor gave me a microphone to speak with her congregation about what God has put into my heart. This was the beginning of my journey to inspire people. She never asked who I was, but felt me in my spirit that I am full of the story to tell and inspire many women and other families. She gave me the chance to speak out what God had put into my heart and it was amazing.

There are people who can connect with your inner sorrow and become part of your therapy. This was the gift that many people have, they do not judge but give solutions and chance to those who seek God's intervention and they do not hesitate to share your gift, your calling.

They listen to God's voice and did obey to accept me in their ministries. Many of the Pastors I met in my journey of painful experience offered their podium for me to share my story. This was a privilege and a huge blessing for my entire life. I was accepted by the church of Jesus Christ, I was welcomed and ushered in the ministries of those He called to share His Gospel. I am humbled too.

I would get a job where I have to start by filling in the gap of my parent's restricted, unpredictable, challenging disappointments in order for us to live a better life than them. I would get a job where I had to start first as a bread winner, by helping out financially to provide for my family, filling in the gap of my parent's responsibilities because of their past failure due to their socio-economic struggles to succeed. I had to be there for my family. My family is and will always be my priority no matter what. This is my constant heart of responsibility that I don't want any person to take it away from me that is who I AM.

Family is very important to me and I admirer and respect every family that strives to become united no matter what, through thick and thin; as married, as mothers and fathers; brothers and sisters for the sake of the generation to come in order to live a legacy of a peaceful, united family. I had to give more attention to their situations than mine. This kept my family from surviving.

My family's life progress is an honour and I have proven it to date. We may have some ups and downs and we still believe in family support, care and love. You cannot build the community or the nation if you do not start by fixing the problems in your family. Deal with yourself first, and then family, the rest of the world shall follow. If you win respect on your family, it will be easy to fix, solve problems in your community, nation or even at your work, business, church environment and anywhere in the world.

My family belongs to the status of my achievement, being in a bad or good books can also tally the image of your family, some of us are chosen to build up our families, to be strong and role model to some of the individuals in your family; to bring solutions and be used as a key to their success. You can be chosen and called as a leader in your family whether being a male or female, you are born with it, accept it because there is a reason why you and it is God's purpose.

Whether you are young or old; physically or mentally disabled, God can still give you this kind of responsibility for His perfect will. He will deal with your character if you miss the direction of your purpose; He will make sure He guides and directs you.

I will work hard without resting enough, using any opportunity that I could get to increase my income, for me and my family socio-economic lifestyle to improve; by the time I had to do my own, personal things; there will be many challenges to face before I can achieve what I want because I didn't prioritise what I want first.

I reviewed my family and my personal achievement for a better life and did set up my goals to achieve. How I grew and treated in the past was not fair and had to be over.

Having a child was not a priority; getting married also was not a priority but it was a wish that remained inside of me; I had many fears and did not want to see my child going through what I went through and or have a marriage that will fail, I was afraid to risk in of this goals.

I had many fears of getting involved to someone who could treat me badly. I didn't want to experience what my late mother has experienced in her marriage. Today I believe in love, marriage and kids. I had to work it through counselling. Hopefully, I will meet someone by God's perfect will. What has happened in the past remains in the past? I am now living my purpose.

All that I want and wish for to date is the successful story of my family. My social and spiritual maturity was also affected internal; I was confused to understand who I am and where I wanted to go. What I wanted now, was to fulfil my family's needs in support where I can. I have to ask God if this was my purpose to live for my family and not for myself. I would feel peace, and confident enough to see the progress that they comparing from their difficult past experience. I would be fulfilled and proud to see individual life progress in my family.

My family fought to become successful and this is an ongoing life progress. We believe our lives will continue to improving every year, with the support from each other. I was confident that one day we will celebrate our success together as a family. Our bond is improving and growing every day.

I wish and pray that this should happen to all other families that are broken by the past painful experience. All that we all need is to work on it, fight hard for it and overcome every stumbling block and obstacle that destroys our families and to build a family that is united; hence it will be transferred to the entire community. We need to work on our past family issues and grudges, stand in that gap to facilitate peace, to build a united, happy family and a community with peace. We need to fight against anger.

I had reviewed my life, do introspection, to work hard to bring change in my life was not easy. I call this experience, self-realization process, where I had to do personal introspections and to allow God to deal with my character. These processes did define my true-self; my personal identity was challenged and restored and I became a beautiful, strong, hardworking and intelligent human being.

After every life experience, it is where you realise that your happiness comes first. It is where you realise that you have personal staff that you need to attend without family or their assistance. You need you to face them and deal with every aspect of life no matter how challenging it can be. That is the reality of your life and the decisions thereof are crucial. I am a giver but I had to control my giving heart to where there is a critical need and prioritize how I give or offer my help to other people.

I wanted to become a better person for me without my parents or my family, friends and community; for the benefits of my personal fulfilment as an individual and deviating from all the negative perceptions about my life. It was not easy but it was worth it.

Some of us, we became bread winners for a long time and it never ends. The challenge is when you forget to know who you are to can enjoy life for yourself apart from helping out your family members or any person.

My salary was for my family to survive poverty; because it was my responsibility to do that and compromising what I first want before me. I was their strength and so is my mother, but my life was around them, their needs and their happiness. I did not want them to experience more pain and I also become a counsellor of their situation. We are now Counsellors to each other.

I was brave enough to protect them physically and emotionally even it was draining my strength, I knew deep in my heart that I had to do. That is why after my mother's death I felt that I do not have life because my life was around her and her past pain. I wanted my mother to see me in a white wedding gown; I wanted her to see my kids like my other sister's children but God had His own ways and thought about celebrating her life by becoming a testimony to the world.

That was my wish but God had His own plans. I was this responsible child; accountable to every activity that I do and any event that was taking place in the family. I had to also build defensive mechanism when things were going wrong to protect my family. Their challenges were mine and I had totally forgotten who I was and who I am for them to see positive things in their lives and my life.

They will also look up to me with hope and a huge trust. I did it by God's grace. I had to work hard to build trust to my family. We share a lot painful experience. We do have our own differences but there is always a solution to every problem that we encounter as individual members and as a family. Everyone changes everyone by how we act positively towards each other and a change comes from the heart when you are ready to change.

Charity begins at home and my family will always be a blessing to my life and how I became successful, will be their contribution too. I had to learn to take care, love and support them as much as I can, before I can be able to support other people besides my family. This became a norm to all of us and to our children.

My family life is interesting and enjoyable to can be part of it. I will look at my age and compare it to what I have been experiencing; and it was tough for someone at my age to experience such many challenges and overcome them. I was in a furnace every year. God was training me. I had to have a story to tell, to inspire and encourage the hopeless hearts and broken families.

I was; I am a refined gold like my name. I had to be pruned like every tree to produce more fruits for a right season. I always had courage in every situation for it to change quickly. Some people would take my patience and I had to manage it before I can do or say anything stupid. Deep inside my heart, even today, I still know that I am the strength of my family.

This kept me going and made me a valuable member of my family; this has made me to make a positive impact to families that I have consulted with. Now I have the strength through God to sustain the legacy of my late parents. I am no longer alone as I used to think, he was always there for me but I could not feel Him.

Today I could feel Him, His signs and wonders. In His presence I will always remain. I am happy with the position that He gave me today and His assignments are measured according to my strength.

My family loves God and we are all depending on Him and He is taking us far where He wants us to be and we are a liberated family of God. We know and are aware that there are stumbling blocks to destroy a strong family, but we are ready to fight against that negative perception.

We have received salvation, my mother passed away as a born again Christian for 10 years, with a strong relationship with God; she left us with the inheritance of clinging into God for anything and her faith and relationship with God made us who we are today. She told us the church start from the heart and that God is our total strength.

We are still surviving season after season through His strength. We fully believe in our Lord Jesus Christ, whom we serve as we also respect other beliefs. He is our blessing and it is working for us; there are miracles that we have experienced in our lives through our salvation in Him. He is our Grace and His grace is sufficient to us.

I have prayed and also preached telling my story and there were testimony after every session. I call myself Motivational Speaker, Inspirational Sister and an Intercessor, Some people called me Great Intercessor after their experience with me in prayer sessions. God has been faithful and kind to every step and decision that I have made to date.

I am more patient than ever, I can listen, I can understand and relate my experience with many people's stories; who I have met and I was able to reach to them and encourage them with prayer and one on one session to date. My painful experiences was not about me, it was a life training to help out the ones who cannot survive like me, who are not strong as I am and who does not have solutions to overcome depression like me. I have started to live my purpose.

My life was around my family and I had to transform it a little, to fit into my social and personal life without them. I was very weak during my depression and this was also a wakeup call to enjoy my life, to find my happiness and purpose apart from my comfort zone of my miserable life, I had to pull my strength for my personal progress.

How we grew and the experience that we had in the past made us to feel secured around each other forgetting that we will grow apart as the time goes on; when we got married as sisters. This is another process of change and we had to adapt to a new life with in laws involved. Three of my sisters are now married and we are trying our best to prioritise some of our commitment besides spending time together. We have gained 3 brothers in laws and 8 children were born in this family.

We do not plan to meet together as sisters often, but nature will take its cause for us to meet regularly. Our bond, missing each other from the heart made us to communicate and see each other whether there is an emergency or not, it is a norm to long for each other and our children are like us.

We will spend time together with their kids. As for me, I am still going strong alone and still being meaningful to my purpose of living. I am still playing my role as a great Aunt, when there is a need and also as a sister or a younger sister. I am so close to their children and it is a blessing to me.

I know my sisters will always need me and I will also need them for ever. My prayer is, to meet a good husband who will also cherish his family and my family in an equal way; and with the same treatment without discrepancies. I wish that we lead with love, peace and unity to build our families for the sake of all our children, the generation of both sides to grow closer with peace and in unity. This is my wish that we should use this as our morals and values as a family from generation to generation.

The devil hates families that are united, he wants to separate them with conflicts and grudges. Forgiveness is very difficult to happen in many families and this can persist for many years. A happy family is a blessing from God. I wish and pray that each family out there can respect each other's position to each other's lives and understand each other's weaknesses. We all need this and we all need God's intervention.

We all have differences but we need to work hard towards building our strong families. We need to learn to protect each other's weaknesses etc. If we do not consider our families for better life, we will give birth to the generation that does not have emotional gaps, emotional scars but a generation that will have a better future to build the nation.

If I do not have love to my brother or my sister, how can I say I love someone externally, who is not from my family; if the love did not start or grow within me in the my home? There is a spirit of affliction that creates hatred amongst God's people and their families. How can I say I love someone if I do not love myself? How can I say I can take care of someone if I did not practice the care where I grew and with my family? Given a starts at home is a blessing hence charity begins at home in English.

Many of us has lost touch with our families, we have lost our identity and our family values. Our parents are living us behind through death, what are we left with, why can't we correct and create a strong family amongst ourselves and forget the grudges of the past? The world is losing its value because of broken families.

I had to learn that I cannot fall in love if I do not know what is all about love, how to love because once I say these words, I am committing myself to someone's character, behaviour and his childhood burden. The question would be am I ready to compromise, understand his weakness, strength and support him in such experiences; hence he had to do the same. It takes two to tango. Commitment is also a connection to embrace each other's joy and pain for better life.

We both need to know and understand what we want from this commitment. It starts from relationship to marriage. Once two strangers connect, it is a journey to commit to what we are both carrying and for our achievements in the future. We need to see the bigger picture of become successful and not to create enemies in the future as it is happening today. People love each other and become enemies in the long run. The question we all need to answer is; why do we meet and love, why do we commit to each other? If we can perfectly answer these questions, then we can make a commitment to each other. Love will remain love; our characters will change how we perceive love.

Depression had taught me many things that are hidden, the emotions and pains that we always suppress and pretend that we have dealt with them; but they can just trigger in a long run, when we are provoked by the people who we relate with. I believe that each and every one of us need to take time to heal before committing to someone who will be innocent because we can use them as an excuse or a healing target, victim to our emotional scars.

For an example, if my father treated me badly when I grew up. I can always be caution and sensitive with any action that my male partner can do towards me if it is a negative action, this can trigger my past experience to his reaction in a negative way; if I did not talk about and heal completely with his support. So is if it was with the mother and it can be from my side or his side. The best solution is to deal with our past and heal completely. It can also be from our past relationship experience that can damage our trust and instil fear to the new people who we meet in the long run. We all need to heal.

The other bad situation that triggered my emotional depression was when things did not work for me where I use to work, how certain people started to treat me with rejection. How I lost my job in the same year as an additional misery to my life, triggered my depression badly so. 2012 was a wicked year, season for me to can remember without any happy memories.

I took a decision to opt for retrenched because it was the only solution to get out of the dark pit that my colleague threw me in. It was already tough for me, and when I experience this pain, I was from the hospital for an internal operation. I was badly hurt by certain individuals and it affected me negatively. It nearly caused me to hate even, innocent people who did not know this plot against me.

I have tried to hate the entire company until I found out it was only certain individuals and a group of people who did not even affect me alone but targeted many innocent people; who were affected by their drastic decisions without feeling remorse. I had to pardon even the reasons of being admitted again in the hospital for depression.

I cannot say it did not hurt; it was painful because I had to be sedated for two months in the hospital and forgot many things, I also forgot many people including their names. I did hurt because I did not have answers that would help me to survive depression.

I was looking for answers from the wrong people, who didn't care about what was happening to me; but to see me frustrated and fully depressed. I was hopeless, helpless and miserable. I wanted to ask these people if they do have remorse by then. I wanted to ask why they did what they did. I wanted to ask God why did He allow this to happen to me after my long years of commitment, dedication and passion to this organization and even in their company's' strategies I was always there making contribution with passion, but could not get answers.

Sometimes some people, can be used by evil in a corrupt way to make the lives of other people miserable, some people enjoys making other people lives miserable and some people are treated badly every day in their homes and in the workplace and it is a norm. I always pray to God for the strength. We are all innocent and created with kind heart but become influenced by the world for selfish reasons.

I had to learn to forgive and deal with the pain inside of me compare to what I have lost in the past. All that I know was, I could not reverse what I have lost in the past, financially, and how I got out of the organization but I can correct how people perceived me by becoming successful at my own pace.

I was treated badly and I became weak to fight for what I believed in. I did deserve what I was fighting for, to get or become what I believed in by then, and the opportunity was declined.

I was denied to prove my intellectual abilities; to make a positive impact in the company that I worked for and I was emotionally attached to my position and to the company's vision and mission.

I became weaker and emotional destroyed when I was not given the opportunity. I was crippled by people who did not understand my patriotic spirit to this organization. I became disabled emotionally because I felt my life, my career life and my purpose was ending.

I was hurt and disappointed. I felt rejected by those who I knew they had a full knowledge that I have the potential to any role given. I still and will always believe I was an asset to bring change and plough back with what I have and what they trained me for.

The experiences that I gained from there, is surviving me to date. I believe one day I will still come back and plough back to my community without any grudges or pain of the past. I am not looking at certain individuals who are negative or against me; I am looking at disadvantage community members who doesn't even know these plot and conspiracy that was created for my position.

This was a lesson learnt in the corporate world and now I know and have the experience of the lifestyle in the corporate world when it comes to positions and performance.

This was for a good purpose to be pruned, trained and refined to become successful, because I am still here to correct what happened in my past with what I am achieving now.

I saw a new season because I forgave all people who were part of these cruel incidents. The fortunate part was I know who they are and recently I even knew why they did this. One of them was able to confess and gave me the names of everyone who was behind my downfall, this brought me peace and I forgave them.

All that I can say in these books is that, this was a lesson to all of us that you get hurt, it becomes an elevation to another season of your successful life; you treat people bad, it is a seed that you will harvest for the rest of your life. Just be cautioned that it is where your dignity lies when the truth is out.

In 2013, it became a year of my breakthrough, I started to regain my strength, I started to go out in public without hiding in my house.

This was a new season for me, new beginnings to build up a new future that I always wanted.

It was a new season for me to embrace new friendship; new people and show case my gift, my calling and my potential. My books became a breakthrough and a testimony to my life and my family to date.

My first book, my life journey through with God became my first deepest cut. These three books are my strength forever and my legacy. I thank God for giving me an opportunity and a privilege to know my purpose to live, leave this kind of legacy, to share my story and inspire the hopeless individuals and families. I was in a furnace, I was trained and I did pass the test to overcome depression; although it was not fair to be treated like that in the environment where I was fully committed to go extra miles with passion to serve there.

It was still an opportunity because I have learnt a lot from there, including to become a leader and a be able to stand in the crowd and address any number without any stage fright, that is the positive impact that I gained from this organization. Any strategic thinking, I was not limited, it is in my genes because of good people and leaders that I met and working with beside the corrupt one who made me their victim to their own greedy and selfish reasons.

Someone once said to me that I got attacked by depression because of the passion that I had to my work which is true.

I was fully committed and it almost killed me. I will now continue to say that it was all about God's plan to move me from that environment to glorifying Him with the gift that I was born with, writing and inspiring. I had to start to focus on me and my family and to the rest of the world without my potential being limited. I had to seek God's face and kingdom and the rest was added to me when I become more submissive and obedient to my calling. This was my turning point, my breakthrough.

This was a reality and a pain to endure that caused me another emotional gap; that was left unattended for a while until it became a painful blow. This was a gun that triggered all the emotional gaps that were left unattended from my childhood life to date. I did survive my depression and had to overcome it with this last lap of losing the job that I ever loved in my entire life.

In this emotional gap, there will always be an element and signs of depression working into our nervous system slowly like a poison, anger, hatred and bitterness. All these incidents are stored in our sub-conscious mind and we will be reminded of why this failure and why our lives are falling apart?

This would also affect our conscious mind, and at the end, it will develop fear of unknown, create trust issues and doubts to anything or to anyone who approaches you whether in a positive or negative way, there is always an element of uncertainty to any approach.

I will start good initiatives without completing them because I was short tempered. I knew deep inside that I am capable to help out and inspire people, youth and women, men etc; even to start business but it will be a huge task to draw out my energy to do these things. I know how to do business plan, profiles and motivate new entrepreneur but my anger will tell me to be alone.

I will switch off my phone when people call me for assistance. I was good in advising people with the past painful experience but during my depression process, the pain will make me tired and I will always feel weak that I sometimes feel my breath is going out my body.

My family kept on reminding me that I am their pillar of strength, a strong back bone in the family that I have played an important role in their lives and they miss me.

They will always tell me that I am intelligent, hard worker and they know I can fight to become successful. They will try their best to revive me. This support also, brought my energy back to stand up and become who they believed I was. I had to follow my dream with all its risk.

My family needed me most for support and advices and all that was in my mind was "I am useless" and why they should have hope that I am important. This thought would kill me emotionally and I would cry until I did not even feel tear drops falling out of my eyes.

I will lock my house and the gates and keep silent, quietly crying until I just cough without tears and get into a deep sleep.

The question was why my colleagues who I trusted did this to me? Some of them I was looking up to, when I valued and respected them. I am so blessed today that my tears are falling now with joy; that what I feel now is so peaceful and spiritual; there is always fulfilment after crying because it is not with pain.

I do not want to experience any sign of depression; if I do, I will work on it, find a professional help for therapy. Talking out your feelings to the right people also helps; to avoid creating emotional gaps in your life. You need to take out your pain by discussing it with the relevant person, who caused it and find peace within, create a perfect time with guidance from the one who created you.

It is not easy but it can release you from anger especially to married people. Whether the person accepts and or acknowledges it or not, from your side you have addressed the gap and how you feel and you also need a humble environment for both of you to address the situations that affect you.

We are destroyed emotionally because we are afraid to express how we feel and what makes us unhappy; we are afraid to face the people who did us wrong in the past, we can give them power to their negative opinion; about how we respond towards their behaviour, with a behaviour that will last with pain, because the same people who have done us wrong, can act like they were not aware that they have caused you pain.

They can also shift the blame and justify their case because such people always have access to authorities and they victim do not always have a chance or opportunity to access superior doors to plead their case. I was left without intervention and what was said about me prevailed than the side of my story that I had for my case at this organization.

Communication is very important to all people who you relate with. That is why, if you are weak enough, any solution can be better for you and you can be sorry if it fails when trying to attempt to make things right on your own. When we survive, we call it God's grace.

There can be attempts to suicidal, alcohol, drugs, sex addict when you are crippled emotionally and not strong enough to fight against depression.

This can be worse if you are also unemployed and you are trying to make sense in any interview whilst you are emotionally angry; even if you have relevant qualifications, you will not succeed, if you are still angry with emotional gaps that are unattended.

I was called a risk; depressed person is regarded as a risk in a corporate company. I had to attend different churches to be revived spiritually. I needed a church with a strong praise and worship. At that stage, my mind would not concentration for a longer period. It was not easy for me to listen to a long preaching but praise and worship was my solution to soothe my mind.

I couldn't attend any service or meeting for long hours. I had to leave early because I could feel my mind bursting and with anxiety, my heart will experience more pain. I had to learn to write the scriptures preached for the day and read them alone at home; this was also a training to prepare me to know the scriptures, as an additional compliment to my strength and motivational tours.

I did not give up attending church, my late mother used to say, the church starts within your heart before you can do fellowship at attend a physical church, you need to prepare your heart first. I started to attend church services during the week and gradually I fought my concentration, and train my mind to listen. Pastors of churches that I visited were very supportive even though some where no aware of what I was going through. I did not share my story my painful story with them.

I would feel a sense of belonging when I am recognised and given an opportunity to share my spiritual experience when I am attending all these churches that I visited. They were all incredible to revive my spirit; I admire them and appreciate their contributions during my depression healing process.

I still visit them in my spare time; I get involved in their events. I have also been regarded as their annual guest motivational speakers in their churches. Most Pastors did not understand why I visited, until I became a Motivational Speaker hiding underneath my calling and I was sharing my testimony.

I was going through a lot and I was hiding under my beautiful dress code presentation, my makeup and my humble behaviour. It was between God and me, because my family did not understand and many of other people, who knows me and saw me in their churches, did not understand until I became a guest Motivational Speaker in their churches.

God was still training me by visiting these churches. I qualified, I was promoted and I can now stand in any podium to any kind of event and show out my gift. I can be prepared or not, by standing in the podium through worship and praise; my gift will present itself and relevant to the event. My submission, the obedience, to surrender to God paid a lot into my life to date.

My family was confused about me, some pastors preached that going to different churches is not the right thing according to their knowledge and expectations, but as for me, it was a different approach and it worked. I was trying hard to find myself a position and not in the church but in the kingdom of God. It was all about my spirit looking for worship and praise; I will thirst to listen to God when He speaks through His vessels for His word.

This was how I became so close with God through worship and praise, through His words I also started to preach and became a great intercessor. Worship, praise and prayer became a therapy to heal through the process of my depression. I also had to learn to meditate and read the word of God to heal emotionally. My relationship with God was renewed every day.

My Lord Jesus became my best friend. I had the teacher of His word, my guider and comforter; I was in the presence of the Holy Spirit through praise and worship. I created myself many families in the same Kingdom of our Heavenly Father; I will cherish that for the rest of my life. These churches that I visited became part of my therapy that has strengthened my physical and emotional being, my confidence and my faith. I was accepted; I had a sense of belonging from all of them.

It became a huge therapy ever. My soul, my spirit wanted me to be there and it will just happen when and where to attend every Sunday. I will always admirer the leadership of these churches, always and it is my assignment to pray for them without ceasing. It is all about unity as the children of God. It is not about number of membership, the name of the church, the size of the building, the Pastor, kind of worship, praise or prophesies and or about the uniform.

It is about the God that we serve and presence of the Holy Spirit; how we respond towards God's word and how we connect with Him. I can represent Him anywhere, preaching His word and sharing my testimony. He is not limiting me and I am not limiting myself either.

All that I wanted was to fellowship not in a church but in the Kingdom of my Heavenly Father without looking at the church name or the Pastor but the worship, praise and the word of God. My spiritual life was revived. I will be spiritually fulfilled when I got home after attending any of these churches. It was not about the church, name of the church, its politics, and or getting a position from the leadership. It was all about my spiritual upliftment and revival because I needed that more than anything.

This was a way of my emotional healing process, a solution that brought me closer to God and I was totally revived. It was not about what people says and their judgement. Whether they saw me in this church and tomorrow at the other churches, it was my mission to reach out and inspire any person and share my testimony. Every Sunday was perfect for me to be where God wanted me to be. I was and I am still comfortable to visit or be invited to any church of God under His Heavenly Kingdom.

I grew spiritually matured to understand all these churches and their role in our lives, not the name of the church or its doctrine. I learnt to respect any church and that it is commission by God for the lost, innocent souls to be saved and revived spiritually no matter how challenged it can be. How I feel was very important and I was also travelling distance to meet new people.

I did not want anybody to understand because I was seeing the results of what I was doing, my spiritual growth and maturity was elevated in every experience. I was a Missionary and I am still enjoying my mission with God, to heal everyone who needs my assistance through sharing my story as a testimony. I have found myself within all these different ministries; I did found who I was through that and it was between me and my Creator.

Losing yourself is the worst failure and a downfall ever if you allow it. I believe we are created in a unique, special way with a purpose to become successful by any means, through our strength, courage and from how we were shaped.

We are all created in a unique and special way, in God's image or His own likeness. I see and regard people as created by God and not by their position or status; how God created you with your life journey should be cherished and celebrated. God still has a purpose with our lives through every choice and decisions that we make or take.

Some of us, we get into commitment, get involved in a relationship with our messy lives before we can even find ourselves, who we are and where we are going; and this is the worst decision ever if we find ourselves doing this. We need to deal with our past pain first and heal completely even if it is a process, we need to heal and fight for our peace, the peace that we were given freely by God.

We all know as individuals how we feel and what we want. We all know our emotional gaps, but we tend to ignore them. We become in denial as we go on with our lives suppressing the pain until it burst with emotions and triggers on its own without control. We cannot ignore that we are feeling depressed. We have to face this attack.

We begin to trust different medication that will only perform a relief to our situation and the reality will bounce back again when we are sober minded. We need to trust our inner selves for a long term solutions, to find ourselves and use medication for temporarily measures; we need to fight the status of depression in good and in bad seasons of our lives.

I had to decide to live a healthy lifestyle that also changed my eating habit and my body weight dropped. I had to go for detoxing process and change my diet completely with supplement and natural herbs. I had to exercise more than ever and once a week I would climb a mountain and do indoors exercise with meditation and prayer as a process of my complete healing.

The question can be, as individuals, can we accept that we are in this kind of situation and deal with it until we overcome it? Are we ready to engage other parties to our healing process?

Especially in our love life commitment, that will lead to a marriage commitment and or having children who, at the end, will be affected more than us as parents; because we have left our emotional gaps unattended.

It becomes critical when there is an innocent life involved because we will be creating a generation of anger and with crippled emotions and psychologically affected.

You can come to a level of adulthood and feeling that you are ready to fall in love with a relevant person but the relationship that can lead to marriage can be destroyed by emotional gaps that were left unattended in your childhood. We all need personal reflections and introspection heal and commit.

Some people will tell you that love will find its way but when you go out in social activities, your friends becomes more attractive to men than you, the question will pop out into your mind; what are they using exactly. It can be your anger, expressing itself in the other way where you do not see what other a person sees in you. It can be a hidden veil that stops people to approach you. What happens inside can manifest or projects out to your physical being.

Sometimes I would laugh loud with my sisters, making a joke that maybe my problem is that, I do not know how to flirt. I would even say I was too traditional to can even seduce a man, the bottom line was, I did not have to use any energy of any kind to attract a man. There was still an emotional gap that is left unattended. I needed to be myself with peace to attract the right man.

I was scared that I will experience the physical abuse that my mother went through. I would give a man a chance to go out with and if I found out that he was cheating. I would be very angry and end the relationship with immediate effect without giving him a chance to explain. I was very sensitive.

It was not even easy to fight this scar and believe in love again. I had trust issues.

I love this depression attack because it made me realise my gift, and made me to belief in love again after reading the books that I have written. I have realised how my love life was like in the past and it was a mess; with these emotional gaps, my love life was under the shadow of Depression. I was shocked that any person can be trapped for a long time if one is not aware of this depressing life.

If you are not lucky and get married at the early age with these gaps; it becomes a disaster when you are not a strong person enough to handle whatever that can trigger your emotions.

When your peers or family members get married, you can be left out and be regarded as unlucky single person who the angel of marriage passes. It is not easy when a year passes by without having someone to approach you and pop the question. This was a blow to my age, where it will also be a concern in my family and people who knows me as if I am bad luck. I nearly got desperate because of this perception.

I had to believe that I am not in a rush and that I do need Mr Right at the right time with the guidance from God.

I had to give myself hope that God's time is the best and not people's time. I do not want to get married for wrong reasons. I will be stacked with someone who I am not happy with, for the rest of my life. I do not care about my age; I cared most about my happiness and what I want.

The worst part is when you do not have kids at that age. The question will still continue with doubts and uncertainties of your sexuality identity and if you are barren/infertility or not. Some of my age group had and do have children in and out of wedlock; I did not and it doesn't matter.

Marriage lifecycle at the proper age said by elder people did pass me. In my traditional believe, elderly people perceived the right age as young as possible to get married. Whilst I was dealing with my emotional scars, trauma and gaps that were unattended, my marital status became an issue.

All that I wanted was to heal by forgiving myself first, understand that my past experiences in the relationships that I was involved in cannot be reversed and I won't beat myself up with regrets. My mistakes can be counted but cannot be changed. I need to move on with my life, attract love now and allow love to find me again in a proper, respectable way.

I wanted to justify myself with pain and this was a huge concern because I felt like I am stacked. I felt I was moving in one cycle of blaming everyone who caused me pain and believe that there is no solution. The answers were right in front of me. All that I needed was to become positive. I had to accept that I have suffered the consequences of thinking that I was in love with someone who never was because of their reasons. I did not have their answers why they did not commit to me. I had my own answers, that is, to move on with my life, learn to become a better partner for the right man.

The professionals will tell you that the decision still lies with you to change how people think about you and how you also perceive things about yourself in the process of your pains; it was all about me and still about my happiness.

I always wanted a sense of belonging and that also lead me, to my influencing behaviour to address my personality in a wrong way. You can end up with wrong or negative perceptions from people who believe they know you better; or know more about you, without giving you a chance to find yourself and you can end up in deep thoughts of failures; just by looking at how you behave negatively to their approach. It was all about getting attention that I am in pains, I am a victim and I need to heal.

People will never give you a chance to explain that you have changed for better from the status of your depression; you have to teach them, it is a process.

You have a mark that can become a lifetime label; that needs a strong character to deal with, how the world perceives you; how to change their mind-set, their thinking or how they see you in the future. You have to regain the strength to face the reality and to correct and fight back your dignity; but through successful story. This is my story and I fought for my life. I am still fighting and will always fight.

There are moments where you will feel rejected and disappointed, this becomes a huge emotional gap that can tear you psychologically and physically. It is when you feel that people are dwelling or thinking that you are manipulating the situation without understanding what you are going through and they would not even give you a hearing.

This is a painful perception that I experienced. I was trapped in my Depression jail and I had to bail myself out in a process where people said I was acting it and I had to go through the trial to overcome it completely.

I cannot always say to people, I had depression, what kind of depression and at what stage was I. The explanation will never end because I had to justify why the attack. I use to be this strong person and now I am facing a down fall in all areas of my life, this was my finance, career, business, marital status, family and my health.

It was tiring to explain each and every experience in each area of my life. I was feeling weak every day. I was afraid to answer private calls because I was in huge debts; I was facing bankruptcy including threats to lose my house.

I had fears all the time that one day, it can be possible that I will lose my house which was my last investment that I was only left with; my energy was dropping that I could not be able to maintain it including my car. I had to learn that I had depression and have to survive it.

All that I can say there is always hope to overcome, to change and become a better person through this experience. My story will continue to be told and there will always be the best outcomes out of it. I will continue to share my stories, and not with intentions of getting back at the people who have hurt me, but to inspire and help those who didn't know how to find the solution from their situation and their depression status.

I was hurt by then but I survived and I am an overcomer and getting the successful life that I have never had before. I have forgiven my past.

I believe that, your depression, our depression can get healed if we take the right step forward and be reminded of our past without enduring the pain with positive attitude. All that we need is to take the right decisions by proving this to ourselves and not to the world or someone who caused us miseries.

We have to know that the world will always have its own views and perceptions around our lifestyle. That is the reality to survive and overcome it.

Live with the depression, deal with it, have facts and move on with your new life. All that I know is that, life has four seasons that can affects our areas of life, we are part of the nature, when trees and animals gets affected, so is us too in this seasonal changes. There are times where you will be happy, sick, sad, overwhelmed and with failures and success. These are reality and facts of life.

Note that it is not about you only; it is also about the people that you are related with, they will also be affected and it can be more than you, or your family when they are used to the fact that you were this strong person in past. You, your family, your community and the entire world is affected when you are distressed. The world needs your positive contribution to be a better universe.

It took my family a journey to accept that I had depression, lost my job, lost touch in the area of my love life and that my kind; generous; loving; caring heart was gone and torn apart. This was my down fall. I did fell in this dark pit, but I stood up with new principles, I had to remove the dust in my face because it has been there for a while and it was already a mud because of my tears; I had to wash my face, remove the dust. I had to say to myself that this was just a matter of time and I had to put on my believe system that I will rise again from my downfall.

I am now healed and my family is healed too, their response is always with a smile when they look at me. They are full of a loud laughter because my life has changed in a full positive way; I am back on my feet again and with double portion of my potential like never before. They do sometimes feel scared that I will go back and get attacked by depression and I will not.

My wish is to continue maintaining my healthy lifestyle, keep, protect my happiness forever, relate with positive people and change the lives of people with Depression all over the world.

I will continue to write my books with passion as it is my new gift that I should cherish and thank God for it. I am also in an ambitious mood to have an office combined with, coffee shop, book shop and book club. A centre where there could be daily counselling with activities for patients with Depression named after my late mother. Form a foundation to mentor young people across the countries including young Authors.

This is my aspiring vision. I still want to travel around the world to do awareness campaign on Depression to work with victims in hospitals and with university students who studies social science and psychology. This is my wish and it will come to my attention to fulfil it. My age doesn't limit me. This will be my other successful story in the long run and to leave this legacy for the generation to come.

3

My Story

I was diagnosed with emotional depression. I had to be admitted for two months and two weeks in the hospital, being monitored by Doctors and Nurses for 24hrs. I was under sedation and had to be treated with medication and counselling. I lost myself, I lost who I was and I lost the inner me. I lost my position in the world, my purpose. My mind was gone for a while, it was dark for me. I was in a dark pit of confusion and misery.

I have experienced sleepless nights with tears every day. As for me, day and night, was the same, I couldn't sleep, I would not feel tired unless if I have taken my depression medication. I didn't have appetite to eat; It was not easy to fight back my health to become normal as I would wish and it was a journey for me to recover. My heart was triggered; my heart was pulled out of my body. My value and my dignity were gone.

All that I have was the questions "why? And why me?" this is all that I can hear in my heard. My house was my cave, my bedroom became my coffin. My other negative statement was "IF, what If" but with no answers or solutions came out for these questions, I was helpless.

I did not want to see anyone; if I see my family, my eyes will be filled with tears. I had to see the specialist and be admitted. I thought I was dead; yes I was because my lifestyle was shuttered. I thank God for this wonderful psychologist that I met and the referral that made me meet another woman psychologist who even bought me a book that was part of my therapy. These two women I honour for their contribution to my healing process.

This was an incident that occurred between January to February 2012. The medication was making me sleepy and I became stupor. I was crying when I am not asleep and not under medication that means, I would cry without stopping if I am not sedated. I couldn't stop talking about people who have hurt and disappointed me; when I am sober from medication. I was angry to everyone who was involved. I was impatient, even to myself.

There was no solution to calm me down than having the depression medication. I just wanted to sleep.

My mother, my sisters had to compromise, listen to all my complaints; they had to support me to go through the agony and overcome it. I was without forgiveness but my heart was occupied with pain after pain; I was filled with the spirit of hatred. My life was torn apart. Losing my job triggered all the emotional gaps that were left unattended back from my childhood.

This was a painful experience for me and I do not wish that anyone who I know, to go through what I went through. I do not want to see any one whom I know to go through depression. I pray for all people who are diagnosed with depression for GOD TO INTERVENE IN THEIR SITUATION AND BE HEALED. I am a victim and now I am a Depression activist.

I was broken into pieces with shame and embarrassment. The worst incident is to be frustrated by some of my seniors were I worked, who I trusted, whilst I was in the medical treatment after being released from the hospital. I went through an internal operation before I was attacked by depression.

I was from the hospital when I got the bad news of my position that I have been removed from the current new structure, in the strategic document of the company that I worked for. The painful part was, I was not consulted or prepared until I saw the strategic document. My senior who I trusted so much didn't say anything when I came back from sick leave, it was a shock thrown into my face.

I was in pain from this operation when I was frustrated with my position at work; then the attack of depression came in during the process of my frustrations, which lead to be admitted again in the hospital. I went through counselling before I was admitted and I was diagnosed with Emotional Depression.

It was hard for me emotionally. I was devastated, shocked by the behaviour of these individuals towards me. I couldn't approach this legally; because I was already diagnosed with Depression and was feeling very weak. I couldn't justify my case whilst under Depression medication and in pain of my recent operation. I had to know my legal status and leave everything in God's hands, to fight on my behalf. I had to focus on my health.

I remember praying and saying these words "God, this is your battle and I know you shall reward" It was not even easy to pray. I did become angry with God too, for allowing this people to destroy my career and to destroy me emotionally and psychologically. My mother also told me to leave everything into God's hands and focus on my healing.

I did try to seek intervention and there was a perception that I am manipulating the system and had to give up my defences. All that I needed was someone to intervene, hear me out and give me the right answers but nobody came to my attention. I was tossed around before I could get the right answers.

I attempted to resign three times, and it was rejected because one senior stated that I want to create a constructive dismissal case, then I opted for retrenchment at the early state of its process, and the response from them was quick to be approved than my resignation attempt.

I was left alone with misery. People started to avoid and rejected me, including some of my colleagues and some leaders when I needed them to hear my case. The rejection was depressing and painful. There was confusion of emotions and frustrations that was pouring in my lifecycle. It took me five years to heal completely; it took me five years to forgive. It took me five years to recover.

I was still with internal wounds while I had to process the healing from my mind; when I went back to work, with Dr advice and not knowing there was already a plot against my position. This plot crippled me to depression. I received the bad news in 3days after reporting at my work. I had to be admitted again to the hospital for depression whilst still nursing my internal operation and this is what crippled me as a victim.

The question was, why didn't my seniors wait until I recover from my operation? For me it was a blow for my mind to capture and carry this said news with immediate effect, whilst I was still settling for my duties to run with. The frustrations and misery started between the months of December the 19th 2011 to January 2012.

My Christmas holidays and New Year was doomed with anger and anxiety of what is coming for me in the New Year, all these questions were in my mind when people were celebrating this season. Back in my mind was, what is going to happen to my job, and my health status. 2012 was the year of my misery, frustrations, sorry and deep mourning.

There were stories with allegations and accusations that I could not justify, I was unable to can build my case legally and or to justify myself because I was in the medical treatment from my operation and now for the depression. There was also a perception that I am manipulating the system and the process of the company. Who was I to can do that, I was just an ordinary employee.

There was also a perception that I am acting this depression and faking it, that it was not a diagnosed status. The painful question to me was, can I risk my health with these medical processes and put myself into debts that I was already experiencing and manipulate whilst I am in charge of all payments? My medical aid was already exhausted from the previous or the first operation and I was adding cash to the total balance outstanding for the first operation and the depression admission.

This was also crippling my family financial status. My passion and the love for this company were destroying me. The other question was can I put myself into huge financial debts whilst I already knew that my job was at risk. I wished for merciful people to come and intervene with no avail.

My progress of healing was also disturbed by these allegations and accusation. I could not defend myself but to be quiet and ask my mom every day, to what have I done to these people who were involved in destroying my career. I kept on saying life is not fair and that God does not love me at all; to allow these cruel people to take me up and down, tossing me around without giving me proper decision about the status of my work and position. This was a life torture and it made the progress of my healing worse.

Today, I am laughing, because when I am reading the correspondence that I wrote during this experience with these people, they were written with confusion, anger and with pain and the sentence construction was bad. All that I needed was to heal, understand and accept how bad things came towards me.

All that I wanted and asked for was; to be released fairly from my duties, properly according to HR policy without begging and requesting a resignation letter 3 times before I could get it. Not to struggle to acquire for early retrenchment. I did not deserve the frustration from these people before I can leave the company and this is what I pleaded.

They needed to build a case of dismissal and I had to defend myself in that meeting and told them that I am going to record the meeting that I had with them and the meeting was adjourned without a way forward but experiencing frustration before I could be released from my duties.

The allegation was not found and they even perceived that I will build a legal case for them because of their bad treatment towards me; hence they were declining my resignation. It was also tough for my retrenchment process and it became personal to some of the seniors. I kept on asking myself why it should be like this. Why this torture, what have I done wrong to this people not to run this process smoothly for me and get released?

They were killing me emotionally. All that I needed was the right answers that I could not get. I needed a decision from them to be released from work, my duties and part ways with this company because what they have already put me in with my health status was already affecting me emotionally and without remorse and or someone hearing me out.

I needed right answers that I couldn't get from anyone including my senior who I was directly reporting to with no avail.

I was writing what I felt with emotions, pouring out my frustrations with confusion, my tears rolling with pain inside of my heart, without even considering or evaluating the contents and the grammar of the letter that I wrote to my seniors.

This is the emotional scar that took long for me to get healed that other emotional gaps from my past. It took 5yrs to heal completely from all my emotional traumas and gaps that were left unattended. I do not want anyone to be treated like this and or to go through what I went through in any corporate environment.

I was betrayed when taking the history of this plot and my attack for my career started from 2008 to 2011, I was seeing the sign of the rejection and frustrations from certain individual seniors but I was ignoring them thinking in my mind that I am strong and I could defend myself in the long run; and this became worse.

I could not hold my emotions anymore. I was fully rejected and disappointed by the working environment, the corporate world. I was emotionally torn apart without empathy from even those who I thought knows me and my history of commitment and hard work. I was facing a challenge of setback, hardship, limitation and frustrations.

I was disqualified by the people that I trusted for my career growth and promotion. My expectations were raised and dropped like a lightning in my face. I was loyal and committed to can deserve this kind of treatment with pain and rejection. All that I wanted was to get someone to hear my story and intervene in my situation with no avail.

All that I have communicated was, to find the reasons why I was demoted as according to the document that was thrown into my face and with no answers when I asked in that meeting that I was called for. I was asking why my position was removed from the structure without proper consultation, why by then the appointed consultants, did not have my Curriculum and relevant documents as it was submitted as per the senior's request. Why their report is stating that I do not have qualifications.

I have submitted all documentation to the relevant person in the administration through email and as hard copies together with those that were of my other colleagues. My relevant documents were misplaced intentionally including my qualifications.

The documents for my other colleagues were there with consultant and with positive comments. My colleagues knew their new positions and the structure prior to the meeting. I was the only one confused with the sad news.

I found out from the consultants who were in charge of the process, that none of my requested documents were submitted hence they stated that I do not have qualifications in their report. This made me more frustrated because I had a proof that stated that I have submitted all relevant documents and it was too late for me to fight, as the submission was made and given as complete; with recommendations, as I was told that the report is send already to the leadership.

No one could help me including the person I was directly reporting to. This was a plot and a huge conspiracy that nearly killed me or destroyed my career. I was feeling weak, hopeless and helpless.

Any perception that is negative ran into my mind and I believed, it was personal and the why? This kept on frustrating me. I could not get the answers. I could not even blame the consultant because they did not know me, they were working on what was given to them with recommendations; but I had to blame the person that I was directly reporting to and also some of my seniors who were involved.

Unfortunately these became too personal with confusion that I became frustrated, miserable, emotional depressed. This experience triggered all the scars of my past emotional gaps.

My direct senior would refer or send me to person after the other without giving me answers to understand why this was happening to me. I was losing my strength and becoming weak. The other one told me at the end after struggling for two months to find answers and solutions that my position was redundant during the meeting that was supposed to be a dismissal meeting for me.

This was a blow and I would ask myself why did it take them long to tell me this in the first place and release me from my duties as I have requested. What case did they want to be built before they could release me? This came after I came back from the hospital from depression therapeutic process. I had to resign after hearing this response and still my resignation was declined three times until I opted for retrenchment due to my health status and the best option for me.

I am not angry at all even when I was writing this book but it was indeed a painful experience that has ever happened to me. I left that company with shame and embarrassment. I become laughter to the environment, my value and dignity went down into the drain because of how I was treated before I can be released from my duties. I felt futureless.

Looking back at how passionate I was, hardworking, pushing to become a competent and productive employee, this was taken away like a lighting that stroked me internally.

I was left with the scar of emotional depression. All the years of pursuing my career became doomed. They faded into a shadow of shame and downfall. I was disqualified. My career life ended because of three individuals in the company who I believe they had they own reasons to treat me like this. Today, this painful experience became a blessing. God did restore my life and He has qualified me to a level that was beyond my expectations.

I am reminded by this situation every time when I go through financial challenges. All that I know is, I was with God through all this painful experiences and that God had a better planned position for me in the future. Today, I believe, I was in life experience training; I have passed the test and trails. This was an eye opening to the reality of life, hardship, setback, limitation to make me a new person with boldness.

I had a vision based on my performance, my passion and determination to work hard to contribute fully with commitment to this organization; but I couldn't get that little last chance to go beyond their expectations for their organizational strategies.

The fact is the truth about my position and why this position was not clarified, instead of getting the answers, the person perceived that I wanted to go through a legal process to fight the organization as a constructive dismissal.

The reality was, I have never thought of any constructive dismissal case. They reality was, how will I fight whilst, I was weak with my emotional depression status, coming from the hospital, I didn't have that energy, I did found the legal advice just to know if I had the case after hearing that I was creating a dismissal case; and I had legal case against the company; but I was not strong enough to can fight for my case.

It was not a priority looking at my health and my mother who was also sick. My late mother gave me the inner peace with the whole situation because of my health status. She also told me God will reward me in the future, that I should work on my forgiveness process.

She told me to leave everything for God to judge, to focus on my emotional recovery, to move on with my life that God will truly bless me in the long run. It was not easy for me to focus and accept her decision for me but it worked. I had to consider that I am in the medical treatment of depression and need to recover and heal. I could not fight, justify anything, all that was running into my mind was that, my health comes first.

I remember saying in one of my correspondence that 'the battle is not mine but God and He will reward' 'as quoted in the bible, Lord Jesus was my strength.

My only focus was to overcome depression and suffer the consequences of unemployment after. I was in a death row of facing a new life of painful realities from getting salary every month to getting zero balance into my bank account, every month. I had to lose my socio-economical lifestyle for a while, whilst recovering from depression.

I did faced frustrations even when I left, there was the other money that was deducted by the same person with accusations from my retrenchment package that I did not request a special leave during my stay in the hospital, which I did and my Dr did communicated it with HR personnel who said it was covered and there is no need for any additional request to be submitted.

The sick note will cover the special leave and we all relaxed. My Dr also asked about the policy and the HR confirmed that they have my records.

I was there in front of my Dr When she called, but this was not considered. There was also an issue with payment of my studies to acquire my other qualifications which was delayed as an addition to my frustrations. These incidents were not helping out even though I thought I have left the company but frustrations kept on following me.

The other incident was the tax issue that was not resolved to date after doing many follow ups with no response, that I gave up and my family told me to make peace with it and pay it.

The painful part was, the person who handled the case from HR again, communicated with tax people in front of me and they did found that the mistake that was from my company side but it was not corrected and I had to come with a way to pay it; whilst I was in financial challenges. After this painful experience, it was not easy to find a job and to qualify for a job from the recruiters. My confidence had dropped, I also had low self-esteem. It was like people can see me easily or read in my face that I am a depression patient.

I did not have a good reference because people who frustrated me were the same people who were supposed to become my reference to my CV. I would be contacted for reference, and the people who frustrated me were still working in the company that was stated in my CV.

I had no choice but to give up looking for a job. I have never worked in any company than this company. This was my first cut to my career development and experience. The reference had to come from there, where I was exploited and disgraced.

I tried many businesses but it was not easy locally to get clients under the perception of my depression status. I tried catering, baking and selling health products with no available clients. I gave up until I became a Motivational Speaker and a Writer. This was the beginning of my breakthrough; my gift, my calling, my ministry, my purpose to my destiny.

Today I know the truth why some people treated me like the way they did; and it was life training. It was not about the company, it was about certain individuals with their personal issues. I knew I had a legal case that I could have won but I did it for my health sake and for my late mother who was also devastated; and was sick by then and had to pass away same year. I did suffered unemployment to date and do not know if it was about my reference, my CV or my history of my health.

My retrenchment package could not address or pay all my debts, I had to struggle financially and the only thing that survived me was my Motivational Speaking to date till my books were published. At least, I will make some little money to cover some of my monthly debts. I survived to date. My car also survived to date, this car assisted a lot in my travelling to my Motivational tours. I truly survived.

It is not easy to acquire a job to date because my reference was there and the same people who gave me the bad treatment told the recruiters that I am a risk to the corporate world; due to my depression attack. I have also given up looking for job opportunities and started with small business that I can survive with.

I started to bake cakes for people who will make orders using my own kitchen, cater food in events when given the business opportunities and I was also selling health products, working hard to bring income for my economic life and my family.

This was not easy but I pushed were I can to have as little or much as I can. This did not last, or to even cover any of my debts because everything was slow. I felt I was bad luck and I tried hard to maintain who I am and pretend that everything was ok. I have applied several times with no avail. This was no helping out for my healing process.

All that I can say is, I was and I am a criminal without a legal case suffering the consequences of my career. It is not easy but I am surviving socially and economically. I am a hard worker and a hustler and I kept on striving to survive financially.

I had to put positive affirmation in my unemployment status that I am a President and an Executive of my life. I am still here alive and I will overcome and survive with or without a job. I had to believe that I have a gift, purpose to live and God is with me throughout the season and it shall come to pass. I am still surviving to date. This is the truth of my pain to endure but not forever, I had to believe that.

I nearly hated certain individuals but had to learn to forgive and move on with my life, my purpose and my ambitious goals. I am happy it had to happen, it was my season to become who I am and what I am to date. All that I now know is that, it had to happen, for me to learn to stretch out my potential, survive and overcome many situations after all these incidents.

2011 to 2012 was my years to face my difficult seasons and again 2013 to date, I had to rise up and prevail with courage and strength in every situation. I had to put on my makeup, look smart and prevail as if everything is fine financially. All that I know was to present myself professional in every event though I knew inside of me that I had debts, I had no food, petrol and electricity for that day. I was giving myself hope and I will continue to prophesise myself with positive affirmations that one day this will come to an end.

I had to experience where I will not even have R12, 00 for air time but to stay quietly inside my house. It was not easy to ask time and again for an assistance from my family. I was not this kind of person who ask, I was a provider, I will always provide, give even if I am not asked. This was a new life and was difficult to even ask from my friend. This best friend of mine had to learn and he will know when I need financial assistance and give me money without asking him.

It was my season with hope to overcome. It was a new life to experience as if it was a history repeating itself but I refused to become a failure. I was not prepared to lose my job, I had huge debts, my package had to cover every debt, and there was no source of income. The money that I get from my business had to be my daily provision to cover my daily needs and it was not enough.

Today I am debts free and an Author my gift, my blessing. If these people did treat me well back then in the company that I worked for, I wouldn't be an Author or a Motivational Speaker. I wouldn't know I have this gift to pursue and find my independent career life.

I had to hide and fill this gap with my spiritual life although the question still stand, am I aware that I have depression as this was killing me inside, destroying my self-confidence and who I really was, what I want to become and or achieve.

What was left deep inside of me was, the negative affirmations that I do not belong to certain group of people, of this world, I do not fit in their events and special occasions. I was born a slave and I thought I would die a slave followed by the stigma of poverty. Socially I was left out and nearly thought that dying was the better solution and asked God to take me.

When I look around, it was my family and I do not have kids to feel guilty about, although suicidal thoughts was not a best option because of my mother's strength and courage. I was confused and miserable. My vision was doomed; it was dark in front of me. I was searching for a light that I could not find.

All that I know is that I do not fear death to date but working hard to find my purpose. I was lucky because some people who are frustrated succeeded in committing suicide. This was the last option but to prove to those who have hurt me that one day I will make it.

I knew that many people had these thoughts that will come when they are alone and we have lost many people who gave up easily. I do not want to die or fail because of other people who impacted my life in a negative way. I rather blame myself for not standing on my ground, principle and strength to fail in life.

I did not want to be like any of them, because that is where you will have self-talk and feeling guilty about your life. The negative thoughts will come and you will only think of how you are rejected and disappointed, by the world. I had faith and believed with confidence that I still have a purpose. I am here, alive and God will perfect me, God will restore me, I will overcome, it will come to pass and will survive with or without anyone.

The other positive thought that came into my mind was I am not the first and the last one to be in this kind of situation, because there are many people out there who went through more than what I was experiencing and it was a step ladder to their success.

This emotions were very strong and tearing my heart apart, I had to live daily with blame to the people who did not consider who I was and did not even have time to know that I was capable. The fact is, I felt that I was not suiting their personal objectives and what I want to become was not their expectations. The fact is, they did not understand me, and I cannot keep on blaming people to understand me. It is their choice to do so. What happened cannot be reversible.

My depression root cause was from my home, how my parents grew, how I grew and it left a scar that could only be healed by my decisions and choices by living a better life; not what my parent's lived and liked, but to what I want in life; what I want to achieve, and become successful. I needed to also allow God to turn my life with possible achievable goals.

One can say it is fair sometimes to become selfish just to fulfil my life with happiness without compromising it, become a priority before someone's life. I needed to live a life full of peace without blaming people who did wrong in the journey of my life. I could not give the best solutions, but I was stagnant, running in one a cycle of life; and with its consequences without moving forward. I had to choose to continue to hurt myself or stop totally and become a free soul.

Things felt apart when I thought, I was near to get a better career, losing my job still was a huge blow because it was my strength to my socio-economic life especial for my entire family, as a strong bone and a bread winner. This was a huge reality to face, when comparing it to the other situation that I came across during my childhood. I was definitely in my 'Comfort Zone' when I lost my job.

I knew my mother was going to leave this world soon and she was given four months. This also stroked my emotions. I had to be strong for her and my sisters. I was hurting inside. This was another emotional trauma.

I had to breakup with my boyfriend who knew after, that I was going through depression. It was almost a year since we broke up. This relationship had nothing to do with my depression. I had another relationship after him which did last eight months and it did not work because of our different interests. I was single for a year before the attack. I was excited to find myself, when I got attacked by depression. I did not want anyone or any relationship besides being close to my family and my mother. It was very hard. I lost touch to my love life.

I was also in shock where I needed comfort and support more than anything due to what was happening with my life. I had to accept the break up but it was also increasing the pain that I was experiencing by then. All that I now know is, he was not meant for me. The chapter is closed.

All that I know is whoever who I was involved with in the past, we were not meant for me. When someone really loves you, you will both stand firm; support each other through thick and thin. This experience taught me how to love and what love is all about. I also got it in the bible in 1Corinthians 13, that love is kind and patient, it does not hold grudges... After reading these scriptures, I had to understand why the disappointment in my relationships and I had to move on with my life.

Stressful situation can create many sicknesses that cannot be easy to become diagnosed by Doctors. My left hand would cause a huge pain out of nowhere and disturbing heartbeat and a confusion of many negative perceptions around my health.

Funny when I do Dr check-up, there was nothing related to stroke, heart attack. It was the stress and tension affecting me. My health was at risk and my life was also at risk.

December 2012, my other family members accused me for no apparent reason and had to face mourning and my personal situations became worse for three months till February when we reconciled, we made peace with whatever that triggered in me. I was also impatient with them and got easily annoyed by anyone's behaviour towards me; because of my Depression stage. Many incidents unfolded with misunderstandings and I would sometimes feel that I was cursed. I felt rejected by everyone around me.

I was going down the drain without seeing any opportunities in life and success thereof. I felt like I have fallen down and that some people have pulled me down. A reality to face and to live with these painful experiences was terrible. The rumours and negative perceptions about my current depression lifestyle continued. This was making things worse in my life and also difficult to appear in public. The perception was about being in depression or mentally illness. Some rumours would say double depression after my mother's death. All this was a perception that became a gossip and a label.

I have scars all over my body, and each scar, has a story to tell. The one in my right eye was through an old man who was riding a bicycle and ran over my face.

I had to get some stiches with a life time scar... my confidence started to deteriorate, if I remember well I was 5yrs old. Then I got another scar in my stomach from the boiling water when I was pushed by one of my cousin whilst we were running and playing in the house. I was 8yrs old when I was admitted in the hospital for skin crafting. After these incidents or accidents I was a patient of nose bleeding going in and out of the hospital. This was terrible.

When the bleeding stops at a teenage stage, I got sick of this and that low blood, stomach acid and going for different diet because I also had stomach ulcer till I got depression.

When it comes to love life, it has never worked where I could not find a man who can understand me better to date. I gave up love and took a decision to wait until I felt that I was truly ready to fall in love again. I could be easy for me to catch them cheating on me. This also took away my trust to be in a relationship.

When it comes to my mother's life, we grew in an abusive and violent family. We grew performing the boy's duties and roles in my family because we were only girls. There was the five of us at home; we grew taking care and feeding the pigs, dogs and chicken before and after school. I would plough and harvest in our small family farm every year, go out in the bush to fetch woods, water, and cook at the age of 11.

I was taught to wash my stepfather's car at this age but I am now good in washing my car to date. My stepfather was violent and abusive. You will learn a lot about this experience in detail in my other book.

He would beat us until we ended up fighting back to defend for ourselves. This was a way to also protect our mother and ourselves; it was funny because fighting back was to run and throw some staff at him so that my mother and my elder sister can get a chance to run away from him; as they would stand still before him to beat them up without running away.

I was good in creating a chance for them to run away and I would be left with him to fight for my own way out. It was not easy too. I use to hate police and the traditional clang systems because certain individual within these systems were not in favour of us, they told one leader who intervene that they were afraid of my stepfather and his father that they threatened them to assist or intervene in our situation. They could also buy in the police and our docket would be misplaced. We could not report or have a case against him.

We did not have the knowledge about violence and abuse against women and children because it was during apartheid regime. All this toll-free systems etc. were not yet in place and they were not there for many victims of violence, the only option was the police station.

We had to protect each other as girls against our father and rather sleep in the near hill under the tree till morning near our home, where we use to stay until our late uncle would appear out of nowhere and find us; or we could see his car at home and rush back home for his intervention. We used to blame our mother until she left him and had a new home with her as a single mother and it was not still easy.

As a family, as sisters, we had to learn that we are not perfect and have to strive for our independent life; but still have each other, become responsible for each other, together with their husbands, we can are making it.

We also learn that sharing our weakness and challenges, being open enough with our feelings, to each other will always survive us. Together as a family, we will overcome challenges of life and we are what we are; through making an effective communication as our principle without the presence of our mother; but to keep her always in our hearts to survive life. Her wish was to see the bond, our bond being strengthened by our weakness, to give each other love and care through thick and thin.

My potential saved me, personal introspection helped me, seeking professional help through counselling helped, and to talk about my experience with victory as an overcomer helped a lot. This therapy did not help me alone but it helped my entire family; to learn to forgive.

We will have a memorial Tombstone for both my late mother and late stepfather as we all knew him as a father besides his mistakes and negative influence from some of his family members. He was a caring person until they got involved in a negative way. It was an issue, but the bottom line was that, there was that natural love inside of his heart, if he could have stood on his ground and fight his emotional traumas and gaps from his childhood, he could have enjoy us as his family.

We still cherish him from his positive side of his humanity as a husband and a father who we only knew, got close to in our entire struggle. My stepfather was born perfect but he was influenced negatively to become imperfect human being.

All that I have learnt in life is that we are not perfect but working hard to become perfect because of the environmental influence and how we grew make us imperfect. But we need to allow the one that who created us to make us perfect. I know that I cannot change anyone who I met or get involved with but can change my attitude and behaviour towards them.

I know that there is desperation in life when you are a woman, threatened by age and being single for a long time. You need to believe in yourself with or without a man.

A man should find you with principles and honour that you are with respect, you also do the same to that man who approaches you with the respect, honour and cherish your submission to him with love. As a woman, love should find you and love conquers all. Men are created naturally to find us and we are created to connect with them because of how they treat us and cherish us as women.

I have been home unemployed since 2012 but surviving. I had to remove the criticism that I got that I do not have qualifications and completed my other qualification of 3yrs Diploma in youth development in 2013.

The pain and the forgiveness process would delay when I was about to reach its edge, but before my mother passed away, she told me to keep on forgiving and that I should allow God to judge as in His word He says that ' forgive us as we forgive those who trespass against us' when we pray.

Sometime during 2015, I went back to reading my correspondence that I wrote to the company that I worked for, for my disputes and I realised that I was sick, wished someone could have rescued me, and that someone could have given me an ear to listen to my grievances. I had to learn that it was my season to pass through the furnace, with all the painful test and trials to become who I am and what I am today.

There are some things in life that happens for a reason to take you to another level of life. There is a level of understanding in your survival, your maturity, spiritual, psychological and emotional growth of your lifecycle.

I lost my job but had to learn to forgive, I lost my job but had to get more time to be with my late mother as a primary caregiver until she left this world, and to take care of my two other sisters, there are many good reason for that season.

I had to lose my job to be able to give my late mother a proper funeral with all the financial needs that I could manage.

I had to lose my job to move on into a new season of prosperity and blessings. I had to realise that my dignity and value was not taken away from me at all.

I had to lose my job to become an author of these three books, motivational speaker and a business woman who still, will pursue her career and further become educated as much as she can as long as she is still alive. I had to lose my job to break every yoke of my emotional gaps and be fulfilled with my potential. I had to lose my job to become closer to God and with a strong relationship. Nothing can separate me from the love of God.

I had to lose someone whom I loved and who I was not aware that I should share my love with because I didn't understand the role of a woman and man before I can get married or become committed.

I know there was and still someone out there who could not reach out to me because of what I was going through. The men in the past broke my virginity but did not leave me with a fatherless child and did not take away my value, dignity and image of a woman, I am, I am still me.

I have learnt that some men can take an advantage of you as a woman without principles and that there are still good men out there, some need to heal from their past like all of us before the find out what they want and to commit to the woman they chose to live with for the rest of their lives. God has restored my woman, as a woman of substance and a woman of God.

Whether you have a fatherless child or not, whether they left you to marry someone else, whether you were told that you do not have qualifications, whether you were told that you are ugly. You still have something big inside of you that will survive you in a long run; if you can pull yourself up in the middle of your life challenges. God will always…always qualify you.

Whether you lost your job or someone you love, you are still here to become perfect and to live your purpose with new people and a new better life. New beginnings are always there waiting for you to have a better happy ending; because we do learn the hard way and get through to our hope with faith to reach out to our true identity. This can lead us to our destiny. All that we need is to hold on and press forward to reach out to what we were created for.

Just continue to love no matter what, continue to help people because God gave you that generous heart no matter how many times people can.

If people take an advantage of your giving and use you for their benefits, as long as you are fulfilled, do it, your reward is in Heaven. Listen to your heart, that is where God is, and where the Holy Spirit remains, to talk to you, to guide you for a better life. God is watching as a judge and He will fight your battles, do not fight anyone back. Be still, your reward is from Him who created you because you live for His purpose.

I had to press harder and share my story with laughter; my faith with hope told me that, it will come to pass. I had to believe that one stranger will find me a job according to God's promise, as his little voice told me to forgive, that means He has a plan with my life and His opinion about my life will never change. He will never leave me nor forsake me and I am still here to live.

I tried many times, to look for a job and till to date with no avail. This was suspicious and I only got one guy who told me that he could not hire me because someone from my previous work told him that I was a risk when he was asking for my reference.

The question to date is, how much damage did this individual did because it is too hard for me to get a job and my reference of long service is there?. I have tried to reduce my work experience from my CV and qualifications to suit certain criteria for a lower position in the corporate world, with no avail that I gave up looking for a job.

I am still positive and believe apart from this stumbling block; somehow I will definitely be successful. I had to declare positive affirmations that if I survived from 2012 to date.

I will continue to survive financially with God's grace and mercies that are new every morning. I am still excited with the feeling that big things are coming, huge testimony and restoration of what the evil stole from me and greener pastures are coming; better than being employed, that is my faith, my believe system. I had to tell myself that if God wanted me to work tomorrow, I will. Let thy will be done as His prayer says and His perfect will, will be done on earth as it is in Heaven.

I was indeed rejected by the corporate world because of my depression and the reference that stated that I am a risk.

I didn't want any favour, I needed someone I that I knew to hear, advise and recommend me to apply to the relevant job opportunities, maybe I was asking too much, maybe I was desperate because there were months were the financial drought caught up with me.

I also believed that I am still young and vigilant to pursue my career. One executive tried to recommend me again somewhere and unfortunately it did not work. It was a blessing for me to know that he thought of me.

I was again recommended in these other two organizations and funny the people that I met were happy with me that I perceived that I was going to be a successful candidate.

The process of interview would run smoothly with positive response and with no avail to qualify for the position. This was stressing me. I remember I approached one lady to ask innocently why I did not go through, with positive intentions of finding my weaknesses so to improve; and she shut me down without responding. It was painful.

I had to comfort myself that some people are not meant to help me in their successful life, or recommend me to any business or career opportunities. I was left with God to recommend me with His favour and open the doors for me, where no man or human being can close. I am full of testimony because it is happening.

When you outgrow anger and bitterness, you also outgrow seeking for favours from people. You will start to develop a room of understanding, patience and forgiveness, this gives you peace whether people develops negative attitude towards you in many ways, it doesn't matter. I am now waiting for God to direct me, to choose people that I should relate and work with, I have allowed Him to control my whole life.

When I lost the opportunity of this job, my positive affirmation was 'this was not the right one and meant for me, mine is coming directly to me' and I forgot whatever the perceptions people had with my past painful experience. It is my past, I cannot reverse it and or remove it from people's mind but I can move on with my ambitious objective to succeed in life.

This will be an enough prove to me that I am ok. I always know that someone is chosen somewhere out there where I was supposed to get the opportunity; I will always and find peace around it. Always believe in to reaching out to my destination as a testimony.

I had to forgive my ex-boyfriend and all other men who took an advantage of my emotional gaps. I had to learn that they were not created to become part of my life and move on with my life. I know it was painful but deep inside my heart,

I have forgiven them. I cannot fall in love like when I was 25 or 35years old. I had to loosen up a little and to believe in love again, in a different way and approach, with principles, from the age of 40 as matured as I am.

I do not blame myself any more but believe truly, that I am unique and specially made, highly favoured under grace. My positive affirmation is 'I know my time will come and God's time is the best'.

I do not blame all the people who had authority to intervene in my situation, or those who were able to find me a job but could not do that due to what they have heard about me without finding out for themselves. Those who were able to recommend the right position for me looking at my experience, skills and knowledge but they did also look at the perceptions; of my past actions without finding the truth about what happened from me.

The decisions that I took after going through what I went through, the stigma of how I got out of the organization, was still in their mind. All that I can say to myself was, I only know who I am, where I am going, what I want and what I want to be. That is all that counted in my mind in order to remove all the perceptions.

My positive affirmation was, they were not meant and chosen to become part of my journey of life and its consequences. I knew these high status people, who can help me out, but they also had unfortunate mind set to label my past and were an issue that prolonged wherever I was seen in the public events.

I do not look back at my past with pain like before. I am the best friend of my positive affirmations. I am the president of my life and what comes out of my mouth has determined where I am going. I am only prophesising success in my life without fear.

I do not blame friends, relatives, neighbours and colleagues who saw a ghost that is miserable by then. Whether they created negative perceptions around my life; it has to happen to become who I am today.

Why the issue of job loss is mentioned several times in this book. It is because it was my first experience to lose a job, I was scared. I was scared that I am going to lose my house that I bought for investment which I am so attached to, I was scared of my debts.

I was scared of living without medical aid, my policies lapsing, I was scared for my family that they are not going to survive without me. I also mentioned my late mother a lot, she was my best friend, she was my strength and I lost these two things same year. I was scared of a new change, the transformation that was taking place in my life.

One day I was with this lady and she said to me, when I told her my story that; the anointing that is not working can destroy me until I understand you're called for a certain mission, your gift and you potential was calling me to live it, to fulfil it because people were waiting for it out there in the world. I did understand her perfectly. My anointing was fighting me…

Today I know what I have been called for my gift, the anointing for my gift and my purpose to live it with peace. I might have lost many things in life and the people I loved, but I did not lose myself. God is restoring everything that I have lost in the past.

I am called to inspire people. I had to be trained before I can stand in front of people motivating and encouraging them with my story. I know their pain before I can even stand before them, tell them there is hope and they have purpose. I have to intercede without ceasing. I am called to write books that will build individuals, families and marriage including leaders of any status.

I am called and anointed to be a special leader of God's kind, unique with my principles and values, bold as I am to face any challenge that will come my way.

I know, I will still face challenges but I know who I am in any challenge that can come my way. I know what I want, what makes me happy, where to find people who will relate with me in a positive way. I am here because God want me to change some people out there who need my story to encourage them.

All that I know is, I cannot go back, I cannot experience what happened in the past and I will not allow anyone to take advantage of me in many ways. I will never raise my expectations to anyone in the world by I will pursue to live a significant life and live a mark of inspiration.

The best experience that I currently enjoy is I can pray, I can feel the presence of my Heavenly Father. I can feel the Holy Spirit's presence, I am proud of my believe system and I know I am commissioned by God and not anyone in the world. I know there are angels around me, protecting me to understand my daily purpose and run with it. I am fully connected to God.

I am not scared of debts, unemployment, not getting married and not having children. All that I know is God was able to give me what I have today and He has reason why He did not give me other things in my life. I will receive and appreciate what He has given me, what I am capable of doing. What I have now is a blessing and what I will have it will be a bonus.

The fact is, I am still living my purpose. I do not judge people from rumours; I rather pray for someone, I do not allow anyone to remind me of my past, unless it is in a positive approach to can make a joke out of it.

God is always on time....He can delay but will never deny what is in for your purpose. Hold on. Hang in there. Your season of correction is coming, restoration and greener pasture is coming...

4

I had to overcome.....

All these experiences were a step ladder to my success, to become a better person and learn from my past weakness and change for better as a loving sister, big aunty and hopefully a good wife and a mother in the future, this is all that it takes; time and energy to overcome my emotional depression as it was diagnose by my psychologist. I was emotionally drained.

I had to overcome by rising up the standard of my living, I had to stand bold and face my challenges. I became spiritually matured to can face any situations that came after my recovery. I had to use medication for three months and couldn't go back to use it again because of the health incidents of my mother and my younger sister.

I had to change my lifestyle including taking care of my health critically so to date. I opted for herbal treatment including detoxing process with lot of exercise and it worked positively for me that my body shape and structure changed completely.

I had to learn to meditate a lot when I am alone, switching off radio and TV to train my mind to think positive and rejects negative affirmations. This led me to deep prayer and connection with God.

This is a process and it needs commitment and discipline to can achieve the best outcomes. I don't mind sharing my story, as long as I share it with a smile to inspire people and with not just a smile but a beautiful smile.

Other actions and approach that helped me to beat and overcome the depression was:-

- Accepting that I have depression through certain behaviour, attitude and seeking and finding professional help,
- Writing/written a book about my life with inspiration-±450 pages that was my key therapy process to my depression
- Becoming a Motivational Speaker with tours in churches, schools and woman events in particular, being a guest presenter with local radio station on lifestyle issues and sharing my life story on how I overcome the challenge,
- Learning how to cook watching reality cooking TV shows with best local and international chefs and worked on my recipes and started my own Chef – Catering Company,
- Became an independent Distributor on Nutritional Supplements – Forever Living Products
- Attendant Herbal Nutritional Detoxing programmes for healthy diet, exercising on daily basis for 30 minutes morning and evening in my house as a daily routine
- Organizing events with local women
- Attended events to gain my personality
- Maintaining my Garden from vegetables to flowers,
- Organize Dinner/Lunch with Family and friends,

- Spend more time with children between 2-10yrs to challenge my thinking by engaging myself in their activities, especially with all my nieces and nephews,
- Share my inspiration daily on my Facebook page
- My best Novel to read every day was the word of God- Bible to find encouraging scriptures
- Writing different concepts on lifestyle issues and innovative programmes to suggest to different sectors.

4.1. The signs of my Depression...

I had mood disorder, I lost appetite, had emotional and physical problems. Tomorrow I will have headache, my left arm will experience pain every morning when I woke up, I will visit the Doctor and went through nervous systems to check my nerves, my heart was checked, I went for lungs x-rays and everything was negative, until my medical aid was exhausted.

I was always feeling tired every morning and could not do anything. When I realised that my depression was over is when I started to clean my house and do the gardening.

I had to go through the process of healing through medication; counselling and I did it. For me the success was, I was able to see the signs at the early stage before it became worse because some people are not aware that they have it and it go to bipolar stage.

If you see the signs, get professional help and depression needs you to accept that you have it so that you can deal with it. The signs will unfold and the incidents that causes it will be remembered when you are in a process of counselling.

I had sleepless nights, I lost weight, I was angry and bitter even to small issues, I was short tempered and very sensitive; I was always tired and frustrated. I lost interest in social activities. I did not want to associate with people. I nearly became a loner. I was struggling with anxiety and would worry with anything.

I hated gossips, rumours about my situation and what people perceive about it; this will continue to affect me. I was hard to myself and was always feeling guilty of what happened in the past and my mistakes thereof.

I was laughing at myself because I had forgotten many people from my past unless if people reminded me and it was disturbing to them. My family got used to my questions of asking who they are talking about. I lost contact with people. I will remember those who have hurt me and I did not forget what they did to me. I was always indoors. I enjoyed my peace if I can get a long sleep during the day.

My type of depression was with anxious distress; with emotions where I will cry all the time without stopping. I was also talkative and would elevate my self-esteem unnecessarily by talking too much, to hide my depression.

That is where I was criticised for my behaviour. Becoming a motivational speaker was a relief and a breakthrough. This was another huge therapy for me. I wanted to be in events where I will be applauded and appreciated for my ideas and participation. It was not easy but it was a process to adjust with my stage and talking to people.

I had to fight this signs and make personal researches to fight all the symptoms and the type of my depression.

If you can google and make a research in the internet about depression, there are studies that could help an individuals to know the signs, types and cause of their depression that are exposed and hidden; and that can affect you in a long run.

As for my childhood trauma, losing my mother, losing my job and facing financial challenges triggered my depression, I was once diagnosed with hormonal imbalances and I will visit Doctors until when things started to work out; and that is when I realised I have survived and have overcome depression when all these health events were minimised and faded away unnoticed.

I did it and so are you…

5

My survival....

When I looked at the definition of the depression and the symptoms, or causes thereof. I have realised that each one of us in life will and can be affected by this depression through the above stated explanation. The question is, can we deny it? Due to our social and cultural background and limitations; and wait until we are diagnosed? Our kids will have these emotional gaps at the young age through what their parents are experiencing in their life challenges and situations if not attended to.

Psychologically, many people are facing different challenges and depression is part of their lifecycle, and it needs temporary mitigations or it can blows out of proportion, with negative results affecting our health. Once we are diagnosed by a professional, therapy will be the best solution to use to deal with our situation.

We need to see it coming at the early stage and address it soon through professional help. There are many psychologists with counselling engagement and the patient needs to attend all therapeutic sessions. The decision lies with you and it is your choice to live long with it and or to overcome it. Stay blessed.

I do not want to say in this whole experience I was perfect, I was not, I had my mistakes as a teenager and when I became an adult; but I had to learn from them. I lost my virginity in a wrong way, which is why there are mistakes that I did because of being desperate in relationships. I was using the perceptions of married people and wanted to commit quickly.

I was wrong to stay with a man for more than five years out of wedlock. I was confused and did not know and understand what about what I wanted, my own single reasons was to get married, I thought it was my only security in life as a woman. I did not have the right choices in all my relationships but I had to learn from my past mistakes.

I had an option of doing away with depression through drinking alcohol and it affected my health and I left it.

I use to be aggressive and would argue until I hurt someone with their opinion; I was doing it deliberately so to fulfil my ego whether you are a man or a woman. I will cause you the pain to show you that you are a stupid person, but it did not remove my anger. Any angry cashier would find me waiting with their attitude at the till when I am paying my groceries.

I was not scared to be involved in a fight, I did not have a respect for any man because I saw my father, my stepfather and my ex-boyfriend in them; especially if you are a married man and would try to make a move on me.

A married man is a virus to me and will find me waiting to deal with their ego drastically and aggressively so because I hated men who cheated their wives. I am now open with how I feel and ICAN communicates it in a calm, humble spirit and that is my new character too. I am laughing now because it is my past and I was under depression.

One of my younger sister recalls on many past incidents where, when we were doing a review of my historical behaviour, we would laugh loud with tears because it was terrible. This includes my driving skills that, it was with speed and very rough with anxiety. My car was in need of clutches and breaks repair almost every month. How I walk was related to a giant walk with a frightening posture.

I always had a frowning face showing two lines between my eyes and this was intimidating any person approaching me including men. One day this guy told me it was not a solution because they are brave men out there who would not care about my response towards their approach. I couldn't open a conversation with anyone. I was impatient but I had a hope that one day I would change. This was the anger that was raising inside of me heart because of the pain of the past.

I was also talkative. Some time, deliberately so, to destruct the approach of any man who is interested in me. I was less interested in being in a relationship. I gave up love. It was a turn off to most of men and I didn't care.

I did not want to hear them out; I will not listen but talk. I would also annoy them with a funny laughter to turn off those who felt attracted to me until they complain about my behaviour. I was doing it purposely.

Today, when I look back, I was actually stupid, I was crazy, I was angry and the bitterness was flowing from inside out of my belly to my mouth; without thinking that I am closing some doors of opportunities to live a happy life. I felt used in the past. I wanted my virginity back. People and my sisters would see a potential wife, mother but I was less interested. Relationship was a waste of time for me and marriage was not a priority at all.

I now believe that there is a brave man out there for me, who will not use my past against me, who will not see me in the past but for the future, who will see the new me. I am busy learning to be flirtatious as my friends always say I am uptight. I am very open to speak, to be approached and to network with people. It is a process but I am getting there. I couldn't differentiate between a handsome or whatever guy that women will scream for, for me it was a man that is all.

Since my recovery from Depression, I have met new people in my life who have made a positive impact in my life, some of them never knew I went through depression; some disbelieve and refuse when I tell them that I went through depression.

My life has changed completely. I met strangers who became part of my family. I am totally renewed. One thing that I love most, about myself in this entire situation, I have never stopped to be a giver when I see a need in any community member; who I know and even the ones that I did not know, as long as I know the need including churches. I will continue to be a Giver.

I never stopped to love my family even during our misunderstanding and conflicts. People would never see or pick up any move to our conflicts because we have a way of solving our problems before they can persist and or be known by the relatives, friends or public.

Our bond was our strength because we always reminded each other that we are not perfect but God loves a happy family that solves problems. Our support was not about material or finances, this was added when there is a need but our hearts with love, caring was our inheritance from our mother. They know I love them and their kids through thick and thin. My life was transformed to date. This transitional process of identifying my true nature, my identity with weaknesses helped me. I now know myself and what I want in life.

I had to learn to say I am sorry, thank you, and appreciate more than before. I love these words because they bring peace in every situation.

I started to attend events with confidence and would be fulfilled with peace where ever I go. I started to comment where necessary or keep quite if there argument is persisting and it worked for me.

I have made many friends female and more male friends. I still hate to be approached by married men; they are like virus to single women and disrespectful to their wives. I hate it because it also brings wrong expectations to any woman who is involved with them; that they become emotional attached to their lies. If a man disrespects his wife, how will he respect you as another woman? It has never worked. Women should stop hurting each other over a man.

I believe in love, I have opened my heart to love again and believe one day I will get married and have children of my own. God doesn't look at the age but He looks and considers the purpose in our lives. This is my prayer and my wish to become a true woman without looking at my age but my physical health being.

I am also praying for a good, healthy husband who I will feel secured when I am with him, with my past, presence and future experience, without taking judgement over what I went through or my situation. I pray for a loving, caring husband and who represent God.

I pray that he becomes my number one supporter of my personal goals and objectives. I know he is out there for God to open his eyes to see just me. I do believe in true love and soul mate to connect with as friends and as lovers for life. I do believe there are good men out there. It is a choice made by two people to make it work, to fight for their perfect love through God and to enjoy each other for life.

My loving, kind and caring character was restored with peace. This is what I was created for. I started to love the inner person who projected outside naturally; and people started to admire me. I am a new creation and my past is over!

6

My goals to move on with my positive life

I Do believe with faith, that one day I am going to get married and have kids of my own. I believe that my age will not be an obstacle for my husband to find me through God's perfect will.

I have learnt to wait without desperation, to enjoy being single and to have fun and enjoy life without a man in my lifecycle. Age didn't become an issue during my self-realization and had to accept that God's time is the best and wait patiently upon Him.

I had to be proud to say that I do not have a man in my life with confidence and not to say I am available. People had to learn that we have choices until we make the right decision and this is me with confidence.

Whether I get married at the old age or not, the fact of the matter is, I still believe in love, marriage and as a woman's wish that one day I will wear my dream wedding gown; and that is my faith.

I will continue writing books, as this has been a huge therapy to heal from all my past, continue with my motivational tours and inspire as many broken hearts as I can.

I will always work hard to look young and beautiful. I will continue to maintain my new healthy lifestyle no matter what and encourage other people especially women to take care of themselves as one of their personal goals.

I love my current body weight and size very much and actually this is my real body size showing the acceptance of realities of life and the consequence of it. Eating healthy is my hobby now and I do enjoy it. I have to cut many food types and toxic food and eat the food that is according to my blood group. I had to use supplements as part of my diet, this is also an additional hobby with lot of in-house exercise in my bedroom.

Doing gardening sometimes by cutting grass, trimming trees and doing my vegetable garden also has helped a lot. I had to learn to spend time alone with God in a quiet place, meditating, singing loud with any worshiping or praising song. Climbing the hill near to my home also did help just to stay around trees watching the view of my own town, at the top of the hill whilst praying for my nation, families and friends.

I had to use any opportunity to share my life experience with the courage to any group of women that I came across, especially when there is a comment of appreciation to my looks against my age.

I am attending social events with excitement and self-confidence. I know I also have a smile so my smile has drawn and attracted good people in my new life.

I enjoy cooking, baking for my family and friends, doing home duties without a helper and appreciating what I have, counting it as a blessing than what I do not have.

All that I have mentioned is, this new life and new adventures that I will now keep in my busy mind, and this makes me to have more ambitious goals to survive.

I had to learn to survive unemployment through motivations, cooking, selling health products, sharing business ideas, sharing the word of God, inspiring people and counselling anywhere I am. I would do anything that I felt I was capable of and this was a route for me to build up ideas to create a source of income for myself. I survived three years to date. This also made me to have an open mind of what business I would have in the future.

I became so creative with new food recipes and got compliments although I didn't go for cooking lessons.

All that I believe in was, besides having a permanent job and certain qualifications, I was still created and born with unique capabilities that can survives me financially in a long run.

I knew that I have many gifts that I need to realise out of my interest and what I love doing most.

I know from the bottom of my heart somewhere and somehow down my life experiences I could have given the negative thought a chance; to have a quick solution to my challenges; that is becoming suicidal, alcoholism, drugs abuser, prostitution etc. and even getting married to a wrong man because of desperation. I thank my Creator that I took a decision to have a positive self-talk and to confirm to myself that I am still here and alive. That means I still have a purpose to live and can change my life completely to become a living testimony.

The best novel that I read was the bible comparing my story with the ones in the bible and understand that I will always have a difficult season to face and overcome. That also taught me that it doesn't meant God is not there with me but to have faith that it shall come to pass. I also read some inspiring books that strengthened my relationship with God.

Getting to know more about myself and learning and accepting that I do have a different character from other people, that I have my own weaknesses and that I need to accept who I am; also made me to understand that my family, friends and anyone in this world also is not perfect but we all work towards to become flawless BUT God who created us will always make us perfect, we are actually perfect in His eyes with a purpose.

I know people has to learn to know the new me, my family are always amazed in how I take things to date, accept how things come my way, acknowledge with a smile to work hard for best solutions without engaging myself into squabbles.

I have learnt that there is always a reason to anything that happens to us in life and there is a process to survive and overcome. It can be sickness, death, bankruptcy, rejection, disappointment, loss of a partner etc., it is still a journey of our life and a story to tell.

All that we need is to gain strength during these processes and rise up to another level. There is always positive elevation to every hard season, where we become promoted to be better persons with inspirations, to tell a story like me, to become a testimony to those who were witness of my downfall.

All that counts was to forgive myself and those who have contributed negatively in my life ...with a smile.

I know I am still going to face life challenges but I have matured and will face them with different approach, with courage and will definitely over come as long as I am still alive and believe that I have a purpose.

Look, I am not married, do not have kids, there will be challenges in this journey too and many more and my faith tells me I will definitely overcome. All that I need is to have a mentality to count what I have achieved more than of what I didn't achieve and regard it as a complete life to face with all or any consequences.

My positive affirmation is 'Continue to strive to succeed, to become happy, have peace and love as much as I can', share and be a giver to any need that my spirit lead me to assist with. I am a Princes and a Queen to prevail as my creator has called me. I will prevail and continue to prevail...

7

My personal poet and quotes to overcome my depression

You can also get them through my facebook page

*T*his was my emotional expression in every situation that I was faced with and the more I share it, it became a therapy in my life and hearing the response from people would give me hope that everything will be ok and this increased my faith that one day things will be back to normal.

I know the below phrases, will help someone to find themselves, those who are poetic will connect, those who are musical artist will connect and write songs to continue to share our feelings, hopes and to those who are motivational speakers; they will get courage to inspire more people out there. I know I am sharing my story to encourage those who have they stories to write them, it is a therapy.

Sometimes we feel sharing our stories, the world will judge us based on that, and not all the people will link your story to your personal behaviour.

Only the ones with fears of unknown will put judgement and negative perception around it but, as for you and me; there is a lesson learnt, there is maturity gained and you will never be the same as your past says, because you took a decision to heal.

It is a process to heal and a therapy; but there are always the best outcomes. I am totally healed and wanted to share my story with confidence. I did not state names of people who impacted negatively or positively in my life. I have my own personal reasons and there is peace around it, why? I have forgiven them. They are my past.

All that I know is that, I cannot go back to my past, I cannot allow any person; any one to rule my life in a negative way. I am the executive of my life and so are you.

I have *always decided to have a good company of people that will always speak positive about life no matter what; I want people with hope so that we bring hope of life to those who are weaker, that is why my smile, not just a smile but my beautiful smile makes me to reach out to those who are hopeless.*

I believe each one of us have a purpose to live positively and we only need to learn how to block the negative things that can spoil our happy life, each one of us has a potential no matter how people can value it as big or small, the fact is. It is your ability to take you somewhere, there are angels out there who will see it, who will make you realise how important you are in their lives, they will go all out to make you succeed and you will do the same to each other as true friends and as extended family members.

There is a person out there who cares about you without pretending; sometimes, our situations can make us not to see such kind of people because we are busy putting ourselves under the dark cloud and or under someone's shadow that is cruel and selfish.

Life has three things to consider when you live your purpose, TIME: should not be wasted on petty things, anger, bitterness and un-forgiveness, LOVE: should be enjoyed with respect, forgiveness and happiness, use your time to love more, DEATH: is the threat to life, and reality. Live your life to the fullest with positive impact and life your purpose until you die, leave a legacy.

We cannot run away from death but to expect it through accident, sickness and other threats, we cry, we mourn and we are left with memories of the lost one, our hearts takes time to accept death but we need to seek comfort from God and those who loves us.

Do not live with regrets because you lost someone due to your miserable life. Lastly BELIEVE: Our believe system should guide us spiritual to overcome challenges, we need faith to survive, we need God to take us through our challenges, we need to believe in a positive way to survive life. We all need peace. We need God's intervention to help us to choose the right religion, leaders and church or any organization as the world is fully of corruption.

We all need to respect our believe system, Jesus Christ died for the world, for the individual who lives in this world and not the church or religion and or its doctrine. We all need LOVE and respect to build the world into a better place for all and for our generation to come with PEACE

I have learnt to go back to God and ask Him about my purpose. I have learnt that we live because we have a purpose and our lives end when we do not have a purpose in this world. I am truly living my purpose.

There is always a mark of achievements before death, the legacy that one leaves behind; the question is what will people say; good about you when you die. We all need a story to tell that will inspire people who are left behind, our generation, and our young people to know that we are overcomers in life.

We can all achieve in life, if we can focus, with courage to achieve our dreams. We all need to fight for the fears of unknown and know that there is birth, there is body decay and there is death, and that this is our life span and reality to accept in the process of mourning.

When you are given a second chance, use it mightily. Your turning point in life is when God speaks to you, saying to you, "I am giving you a second chance to change your life and others, to live your purpose" our God is the beholder of our life and He has also created death.

I want to die peacefully without hating anyone, I want to die being healed emotionally, I want to die living my purpose and leaving behind a legacy. I do not fear death because we are all going to die. If someone can threaten to kill me, I will never be afraid because death is for all of us; the difference is, how we are going to die and when? It is a mysterious ways of God.

One thing that I wish for is to die peacefully with integrity to have contributed positively into someone's life. I am going to leave a legacy of my integrity as a sister, friend, an aunt, good neighbour, a mother and a leader.

Above all, I will die as a woman of substance, a diva, and a phenomenal woman. I know I will definitely make it in life. That is my positive affirmation.

My situation or even my circumstances did not hold me back to what I believed in, what I am capable of and to what I cannot achieve. I did not allow my past to determine my future. I am blessed to have survived depression.

I have seen my parents going through challenges and trying their best to protect us, especially my late mother, it was not easy for her, she had her own mistakes but it doesn't give me an excuse to use it against my failures or mistakes. How I grew, is regarded as my past, what matters now and where I am going counts most. My mother passed on, she is not here today but I am here.

I can even correct where she couldn't, I believe she would have been proud of my achievements. I know she could have done more for us and our children. Only God knows why, I have change the other side of our family life from poverty to success together with my sisters.

We all have a story to tell. Let us continue to inspire others through our personal experience and leave a legacy of changing lives of our young people and those who are disadvantaged. We can stand the challenges we are faced with every day.

Some people commit suicide, I am blessed it never came into my thoughts. Some people go into prostitution, drugs and alcohol, they all need us to tell them they can survive and not to judge them, they have their own emotional gaps and traumas. They were created and born with a purpose and perfectly so until the world took away their nature.

All this experience is the impact or the cause of depression. We even shift blames instead of coming up with solutions to our problems. We have broken families because of depression; we have angry leadership, society because of depression. We all need to fight it, heal and build a better world for the coming generation that will understand the meaning of peace, love, forgiveness and caring for each other. I cannot continue to blame them. Some answers of why we were living like this, are dead with them.

I cannot blame them forever or I will move in one circle of life with blames or shifting blame and giving excuse to suit my failures and mistakes directing them to how I grew and to my parents. I know I can change the generational curse of poverty or struggle by living a better life and understanding my purpose. I can change how the world perceives my parents, my childhood background by becoming successful. It is our turn; this was my generational season to change the life of my family for better.

I cannot blame my past now, I am in the present and working towards my future, whatever happened is irreversible, I am not immortal to can change what happened. The issue here is to correct, learn and forgive.

Forgetting is another thing because there will always be a scar of all the accidents and incidents that took place in our life journey, what we need is to accept that they happened for a reason but we are still here to move on with our new life, new beginnings and make a provision to meet new people.

I wanted and wished to move from the environment that I grew in but one thing that came into my mind was, even if I move with the attitude of forgetting everything of where I come from, I was lying to myself until I decided to face my past, deal with every trauma, so when I decide to relocate to any country, it is not about running away from my past pain but as a decision to my success.

Success is a process; I had to earn it through hard work and pain. I had to work for it, I had to dream it, eat it, walk it and live it. I had to dream success to achieve some of my goals and forget my past pain.

We all need to strive and try hard to handle all these past memories for the sake of our well-being. I was in the edge of giving up, God intervenes. I do have the scar of my past pain. I do not want to scratch this scar because it can be a wound again and my forgiveness will be meaningless.

There is always a compliment to each experience being negative and or with positive impact.

All that matters is my heart and health before I become 50yrs old. I will be stable, but I have to start now to take care of myself as a good, long term decision. I have to take care of myself so that I do not experience more pain at the old age and die with unforgiving heart, anger and bitterness.

All this issues are health hazards or risk in our lives e.g. Blood pressure, diabetes with heart disease, depression and other chronic disease. I am making myself happy with the little that I have and making other people happy too.

I had to know my purpose and live it. I have allowed God to use me differently. I had to understand my gift and my calling to make positive impact in other people's lives. I met strangers who were generous to me.

I had to be careful of what I say because anything that I can say can make people to perceive me either positively or negatively. I have to watch my tongue carefully. I had to enjoy the company of good, positive people and enjoy my life. I also realised that I have sense of humour that was unnoticed in the past. I do not want to be desperate for anything but to take life easy and note that easy come and easy go…easy go and easy come. This is one song by old time musicians.

Anger and bitterness is our enemy to depression, for the depression to leave you, it is a process and one has to make a drastic decision to overcome it. Once you are diagnosed, it becomes a stigma, it gives you a label.

If you do a mistake, it will definitely be linked to your depression status, it will be a form of excuse for people to degrade you and deny you opportunities by any means. It will destroy your image and demote you somehow, the question is, are you going to allow it to be like that and for how long?

The world and I meaning certain people wanted to begin to put my actions together and label me in many ways to suit their personal objectives, agendas, positions and status, but I had to stand up boldly and ratify their perceptions by finding my inner self and my potential.

2013 year-end holidays, I spend it with my loved one and it was fulfilling, my heart was filled with happy memories, this year was my year to process my forgiving heart to reality, it has ended with happy memories ever. All that I can say to myself, friends and family was 'we did it, we have crossed over to new things, we were ready to press on, move on and hold on to our dreams, goals and purpose to reach our destiny.

This was a step to our faith and that year we did achieve some of our goals and it was fulfilling not to have someone admitted in the hospital.

I thank my family because they had to learn to stand for me and support me throughout, their kids where there for me and became my best friends as young as they are.

My family was, they are still very protective, and they do not want to see me hurt. They are also sensitive to who I associate with, it is because of what they have witnessed during my depression trials.

I have always spend, almost every day with them especial my other younger sister, crying and sharing a lot and laughing a lot through thick and thin.

She is the one who was very close to have my daily experience of my depression; from home to hospital and coming back. She was also affected, it was a trauma to her, and she did not want to lose me. She saw a lot of my daily painful experience and challenges. It was heavy for her emotions too.

Overcoming depression was and it is a huge testimony to all my sisters. They always say, they knew that I was going to fight it because I fought for many things since our childhood and succeeded.

My family showed me they needed me more than anything one in the world and that life without me was going to be empty, so I was a blessing, which is what also kept me surviving.

My family is my strength, my sister's children kept me going every time I see those performing good in their education. I am their mother too. I always tell people I have children because I know and it is always in my mind that If something happens to any of my sisters, I am the direct contact and their children are mine to for their growth and I have learnt to have a bond with them from their birth to date.

I am privileged because I am always with my sisters at the hospital when they were giving birth to their children. This makes me a proud, aunty -mother.

I am also a mother to all people who I had Counselling with; I am a family and a sister to couple and families that went through my Counselling session. As for me, this is my legacy.

The health progress of my other younger sister, made my relationship with God to go stronger every day. We all survived. She is also a huge testimony to my family.

Forgiveness is a process but we do not need to allow the process to prolong. God has forgiven us many times. We all need to forgive each other and find peace within ourselves to survive life. I know my mother will and was always proud of my hard work and self-determination.

My family used to say, I remind them of my mother, her courage and hard work to look forward in every situation in her life. Actually all of my sisters, we have the same genetic element where we draw our strength to pursue success, when there is no hope and we fight to create it. Every time when we share our challenges we think of how our late mother fought for her dignity and value in her family and community.

We know we resemble her natural positive courage and patience in everything that we do or decide on. We are indeed successful today because of her prayers, we have faith because of her faith in God, and we forgive because she had a forgiving heart, and we are always and we are what we are because of her.

There is a season, where you feel you are crushed, broken and falling down, without seeing a light or positive things coming your way. Ask me, God was right there with me.

He was with me, in me in that desert of depression, in that storm. He was with me, and in that battle. He was fighting on my behalf, He was in me and with me, and His spirit was upon me.

I did not give up, I fought back. I had to remind myself that I have dominion over my situation, I have power to overcome and I will never lose my hope to survive, because I still have a purpose to live life to the fullest.

All that I can say is; it is ok; it is well. Even if I can move to any other place, environment, country, I want to go out there without blaming anyone in my past; but I want to go out there because it is an adventure for me and because I am exploring the world. No one will ever make me fail in life but I want to say' I thank them for what they did'

I want and wish that when I get married and with or without kids, I do not use my past as an excuse to my new family but become happy as much as I can. Life is too short to have negative influence and or personal grudges consuming your joy on daily basis. The past is the past.

I want and wish that what I will achieve in my career or business, I should not use it to my juniors or my staff as an excuse to insult their potential and or destroy their confidence, but I want to become a positive leader, motivator and inspire them as much as I can; who will also delegate and monitor for the success of all; this is my new life, my new me and for a good purpose; life is too short to waste it on petty things that would cause many grudges creating a comfort zone of pointing fingers and shifting blames.

These unresolved grudges have stolen the unity and happiness of many families. Families are broken for good out there, new generations are quoting the past mistakes of their parents and capitalise them into their failures.

This grudges are continuing to generation after generations, this is extended to the entire community. There is no more spirit of Ubuntu (humanity) because of broken families.

This has caused many delays and has created many barriers for people to can achieve their blessings, there is lack of peace. We need to change, accept change, review our culture of doing things, change our attitude and behaviour towards each other and become positive. We were created to love each other with peace and not to curse or hate each other.

I never give up, I never embrace my storm, my challenges or my battles to drag me back with fears and doubts. I didn't lose hope. I did not allow my situation to determine my future, or allow people who are used by evil to degrade me. I will never allow any person who doesn't know how to appreciate to pull me down again.

I will never belong to where I believe life is not worth for me to be there to please people. I will always move on without a barrier to where I see positive things happening and use it to my advantage; and as an opportunity to become successful.

I do not want to turn back to where I used to be, my old character is gone, my old me is dead. I am a new person.

7.1. Poet....

Never mind my scar.....

I have a hidden scar; I have a secret of my scar...
All the scars...the story I can tell about my scar...
I am...I am a woman with the scar...
Can I show you my scar...?
If I trust, I will show out my scar...
Beneath my breath, my pain...I am reminded of my scar..
But my scar doesn't defines me
And or
Define who I am inside..
I tried to hide my scar,
My emotional scar
My physical scar remains a Scar

To remind me of my story, my past
This scar, was a wound, that was treated
And remained a scar to be forgotten..
I look at it but I don't remind myself of the pain…
It is my past, I forgive and it is just a scar
A light scar, enlightened by the joy inside my heart
My nature, my creation was not with any scar that I could have…
I am still myself with or without the scar I remain
Myself…
Do not look at my scar,
Look at the inner beauty
Do not remind me of my scars
Remind of my nature… My beauty…
I AM BORN WITHOUT A SCAR…

Motivation and inspirational words….

It shall come to pass

"When you suffer in the public,
God will bless you in the same public that degraded you…
Psalm 23:5 'He prepares the table, in the presence of my enemies
and anoint my head with oil'

Let your enemies plot; let the people close to you make a laugh
out of your situation; let you face the rejection and disappointment,
go through sickness, go through bankruptcy, lose people you love
and let all the perceptions come from all the directions from those
who thinks they know you, where you come from, how you were
raised and fell,

How you lost your job, your business, how you got married
and how you bore a child, how the father/mother of your child
left you unexpected, how you got your miscarriage, how someone

got married to someone else instead of you, how you got divorced, how you were left alone to raise with anger and bitterness, how some people gossips about your downfall, how you were treated badly by your boss/colleagues at work; your relatives; friends; neighbours; how you got sick and people diagnose you with all kinds of diseases and suffer all the consequences of your life without a moral support; it does not matter.

These could have crippled your value, dignity and status for a while; you are still here to live with a purpose, abilities inside you to conquer; and the question still is; who is in you, who created you? No matter what 'Greater is He who is in you than the one in this world; it is a matter of time, it shall come to pass and you will definitely rise again,

It does not matter, you are still here, you will rise again, your faith and hope, trust to the one who created you; you will overcome; it is a matter of time; It will come to pass and it shall come to pass,

Joshua 1:8-9 Amen

7.2.   My personal Quotes to inspire…..

'Your respect and submission should attract real love, love should not be pushed or force to come your way; love should find you and love conquers all'

'Do not allow your desperation to find you the choices to live and take the decision that will invest your downfall, seek the right signs and trust your instinct; your conscious mind can tell from the heart what you feel; Your happiness comes first'

'Even when I stumble, doubt my Creator's presence with fears of this world. All that I know is He is still here throughout; with me. He still loves me; so glad that Jesus loves me still'

'**Speak** *any word with positive affirmations over every situation you experience; God will restore your life.' Ephesians 6:17-18,*

'**In this journey of my life**; *I will have the storms; challenges and go through the furnace of kinds, in do and out of do seasons; the question is who is with me?*

All that I know is that; I know I am not alone in this journey of life with misery; the one who created me /you is with me throughout,

All that I needed to do was to speak His word with authority to overcome any situation; Lord Jesus became the word to my heart, the flesh to my weak flesh and the light to my path *in my life; Abide in me and I abide in you, it is God's word.*

Your word says John 14:23 'If anyone loves me, he will keep my words, and my father will love him; and we will come to him and make "our home' with him" living with God's word shows that He will make my home His home,

Lord, restore me and make a home with me, so that I can speak your word with authority, with positive affirmation,

DECLARATION...

There are many powerful words that you can speak with authority in the midst of your situation,

Just speak the words 'Greater is He who is in me that the one in the world, He will never leave me nor forsake me, No weapon forged against me shall prosper, my curse- my enemies may attack one time fold but will fall back seven times in folds; though I walk through the valley of the shadow of death, I will fear no evil; thousands may fall and ten thousands may fall on my right hand side; He will always command His angels concerning me and guard me in all my ways' I can write more declarations here

as your positive affirmation to overcome your situation; just read
the word of God; speak it with authority for your restoration"

'I was called mommy by the children who I didn't bore but have
been part of their lives throughout and it is fulfilling to be called
that; so emotional and as for me, I count it as a blessing"

'Sometimes, **we** allow the deceitful thoughts to drag us to speak
negative affirmations, rather visualize and train your mind to
think positive, meditate on positive affirmations, confirm these
thoughts by speaking out that 'Yes you can, and say it again 'I am
beautiful, unique and special'

As for women; if someone says; you are a BITCH; translate
it positively and say...

Yes I am,
B-Beautiful
I – Intelligent
T – Tough
C – Caring
H – Happy and Heavenly Special,

'No one will ever understand the situation that you are in, until
they become part of it. It is easy to judge until you experience the
same situation to keep quiet and stop judging. Listening without
taking sides is a skill,

Never judge anyone because you do not know how much they
try, to work hard to remedy and or come out with solutions from
their situations,

One thing that I love most is; the man above; your Creator
knows the truth to can only judge; He is God of hearts."

'**Start to** *appreciate God your Creator with little things as you regard them and He will trust you; Thank Him for that little blessings you have received and He will TRUST you more with bigger things,*

All that I know is; silver and gold belongs to Him above, Have a little FAITH and start to open your eyes to see, receive and appreciate; YOU WILL DEFINITELY ATTRACT GREATER THINGS"

"If you really want your everlasting peace….when evil wants to deceive your mind with negative thoughts "worship" the Lord with all your heart, disturb the negative affirmations with a worship song till you fill it in your heart; just praise and worship; It is a good therapy"

I rather become silent with worship in truth and in spirit. All that I can say to my Creator, Thank you for the things and the new things that you have done to me and that are still to come; that is my faith"

*"**Never asks a lady** 'why did you not get married?? Marriage comes from God's will and His time is the best; wait upon Him at the right time,*

If He was able to give others a marriage blessing; He has reasons why He is delaying your marriage;

He is God who delays and cannot deny you a blessing; there is always reason behind His delays; which you will understand in the long run; so is me; just be still as patience pays the full price; do not be desperate. You are still a Queen/King after all".

*"**I look at every year that passes** and say 'my past is over' I will always cross over to the new beginnings and to reach my destiny because I am not alone, but through with God'*

'If you want to be angry #**laughing**#, *be angry; if you want your skin to look dry and old; do not laugh and become serious always when people are enjoying their laughter.*

Even a baby can feel your heart when it is bitter and angry; that the innocent child can scream with tears, filled with fears,

Angels smiles even when things are not going well because they 'always' have hope that everything will be ok; be still and SMILE"

*"**What your opposition is saying** today negatively about you is temporary; and that is the opposite of the positive things that are about to happen; fear is catching up with them,*

They are sensing that, God; your Creator is about to promote; elevate you,

The enemy cannot just strike when he did not see something valuable inside of you; If He strikes, that means you are bigger and have something bigger than theirs,

So why worry; be still; your God is bigger than them and will fight for you and always; He will also be your advocate; always

Be still and know; He is God"

*"**Saying I am single** does not mean I am available for those who like to take chances; Single is not a status; it is a decision with choices of hard work, independence and without desperation,*

Respect me and your approach also counts; I cannot be comparable; I am a Princess of the most High God who deserves what her Father above invested her with; with or without a man; she can become a Queen in His Father's eyes,

I am unique, special and beautiful; Trust me"

*"**I am single but not alone** because my Creator is my maker, my provider,*

I did not have kids of my own, but He gave me more opportunities to show my motherhood at my best,

I did not have a job but He provided me from my house, clothes, food and I always looked stunning all the times because

He kept me glowing no matter what,

I wanted to fall some times, but you always send angels to pick me up to look forward for your grace and mercies at the right time and it cheers me up,

He did not make me rich but He gave me financial securities, He gave me life, love, strength and hope,

My faith has grown to trust Him now and for evermore, Bless all the people that have made a positive impact throughout my struggle, they indeed true angels,

My Lord Jesus; You are amazing Father; your blood protected me; Holy Spirit, thank you for guiding me; Heavenly Father, thank you for giving me your only beloved Son to die and pay the price for me, I exalt and glorified your name; Amen"

"God will always...He will continue to perfect us because His grace is sufficient to us,

Do not work hard to become perfect; God knew why He created you with the way you are; you are complete together with that weakness; He always have the reasons to what we are, who we are, what we will become and where we are going; just shout and give Him praise because He is the only one who is holding your life, It doesn't matter what and how the entire world can say about you in a negative way; they are always created to become part of the reasons why you live; unless they will only keep quite when you are dead,

Keep living for season to season, negative people are our steps to success, you become matured when they talk, God promote us when we overcome such challenges; stay bold and with courage"

"Ladies, let me share this with you; IF a man truly love you; he will not mind spending for you; he will not even count how much he has done for you because he know in his heart he want to spend the rest of his life with you; for him; he is a man who want to take care of his love,

Men, knows exactly what they want and who to spend the rest of their lives with…and they will go extra miles without counting to get what they want from a woman; they are created to love; we are created to submit and respect them but receive love in return,

A man is created to see a woman as a wife to be or as a girlfriend for lust, or as a woman to cheat with; there are many signs for women to this categories….

As a woman, you chose and decide to become a wife, girlfriend, mistress and never blame this man for his behaviour towards you because initially, you accepted to fall under one of this categories hence men are easy to express how they feel about their relationship with you and instead of facing and accepting realities, we create hope for their change and it never happens.

*"**it is a shame to see your ex**, who dumped you still admiring and stalking you by telling you, you look beautiful and young man, woman, it is not the end of the world to be dumped.*

Someone has to move on because someone out there is definitely going to admirer you for real"

Man's heart is equivalent to his character and knows exactly the ratios to find a woman, girlfriend and mistress for his own ego and status"

*"**Any morning, any day, any week,** any month, any year; fix things; Make them right and find your driven purpose to live; Smile heals and peace makes us to live for long"*

*"**You will waste time, energy, and drain yourself**, thinking of people who were supposed to do this and that in your life; it never*

works; because they did not do it anyway; why? because they have made a choice and a decision not to do it for you...

Stop blaming people who intended to do whatever they did to you purposely,

Just laugh out loud! They were raising your standard to become matured with accepting things as they are, they were shaking you to know that things do not always comes to your way as you wish them to come, but one thing that I know is that; you will never be broken heart for a long time"

"Repent; Be Obedient; be humble with humanity; *Be a Giver and submit to God who Created you; He will give you wisdom and teach you how to manage the world and its submissions,*

Forgive; forgive and Forgive; Let love lead"

"One thing that I will live and die with is *LOVE, i.e. is the LOVE that I have for people who respect me for who I am and not what I am.*

I love, respect and honour any person from who they are and not their position, status, wealth, etc. because that is temporary,

If you are close to me and or my friend...let us respect who we are from the inner being and not what we are; Peace"

"I say these simple words to any friend of mine who need comforting words; Persevere, be Patient, be Still, Waiting upon the Lord; it had to happen for you to be pruned,

A new bud will spring forth; be still; I know He is able, some of you know what I am talking about; some of you do not know but God is able...

I know where I come from, I know my past but they pruned me, I was in a furnace like gold but became a diamond ring and this is for all of us...

You had to go through that and not any other person but you; it is your season to overcome, face that giant, face that storm, face that mountain, God will always make a way when there is no way. He did it of me and for the Israel to cross the red sea; so who are we no to cross over our challenges?

I do not care how many time I will be challenged or fall, as for me; bring it on; I know I will overcome; I know; How? All that I know is God will NEVER give me a challenge that I cannot win, because I trust Him and that He is bigger than 'any' situation we come across,

Say:- I DO NOT CARE HOW BIG IS MY SITUATION, I AM NOT AFRAID; I WILL NOT FEAR; I WILL RISE AGAIN; I AM FEARFULLY MADE; I AM MORE THAN A CONQUERER, MY PAST IS OVER; I AM NEW; I AM UNIQUE; I AM SPECIAL AND CREATED IN MY FATHER'S KINGDOM,

I AM WHAT GOD SAYS I AM; Beautiful/Handsome, awesome, powerful and intelligent,

I am the daughter/son of the most High God, I am highly favoured"

"God will make a way when there is no way, God will correct what the world has perceived wrongly about you; your life; it is a process but it will definitely fades away,

When God has restored your life; no one can reverse it,

Say 'My past is over; defeat and failure are things of the past' Better is not good enough; the best is yet to come and God's time is the best"

"Always be proud of the little good that you have and or have done, make it bigger, stop wanting people to appreciate you; you will raise your expectations and get disappointed If they do not appreciate you,

We are not perfect but learn towards to become perfect and better,

"Staying positive, attracts positive people, *opportunities and brings success towards you; Always; always have positive attitude no matter what; start to work on it…it is a process; the stranger you see today…can be your key to your success tomorrow; so be careful on how to treat people"*

"When you are persecuted, mocked, *rejected and disappointed. Do not hurt or be frustrated, kneel down and pray BECAUSE God is about to promote you, He is indeed taking you to another level; your promotion is coming; be revived for great things are coming, new beginnings, company, position, partner, finances, health, marriage are renewed to those who have HOPE"*

"When you decide to study, *do not think it is only for employment of a better position and never think the qualification will take a lead in your career only but it will also make you become a good entrepreneur to operate your business professional, with all the skills, experience and knowledge you acquire from the same qualifications; always thank the people who contributed to your studies"*

"It is hard work to live different lives and changes your character, *to try to suit the environment that you are in, work in or any social group that you want to join,*

Why do you try and work so hard to change your lifestyle because of social status of other people????? It is a fake life and temporary because If you do not maintain and or live according to their "lifestyle' expectations; they are done with you,

Do you really need that? Just be yourself with what you can and cannot do or have; take your time and plan to achieve

according to your affordable pace; there are times when you need
to win a favour to succeed; just believe in yourself; build that ego;
build that self-esteem from inside out; be yourself. Do not prove
to the world or people; prove it to yourself"

"Women, Let us move out of our Comfort zone *and become*
divas… women of substance; phenomenal women; women of
integrity; work harder; press and push harder and PREVAIL as
Queens and Princess; as for me a Queen is a married woman and
a Princess is the woman who is prepared to be married with self-
respect without desperation but with dignity and value of who she
is and I am one of the Princess"

"Talking bad about someone *who contributed positively in*
your life and recruiting immature people (those who never listen
and or find the other side of the story but judges quickly and
become embarrassed when the truth comes out) to turn against
the person who made many efforts to turn your life into success,
but in return you disappoint and bad mouth them? You are still
touching and mocking the one inside him/her because God chose
them for your success"

"When you chose to fail; *do not bad mouth those who tried to*
succeed but direct the *blame to you"*

"It is very difficult to ask forgiveness *when you know in your*
heart you have spoiled someone's name; especially to go back to the
same people you gossip with and ratify your statement, to use them
for your own personal benefits and that is temporary? It is very
difficult for you and for them because they were easy to judge, this
is facts of life; let us learn to appreciate and minimize our negative
judgement, whether there was mistakes made, the journey of life is

long that somewhere; somehow, we will need each other's help and
God only said 'as I have loved you, love one another' nothing else"

"Just be careful, learn to appreciate; minimize perceptions
and judgement"

"Do not allow your current situation limit you! Say No
to failure and disappointment, you are the child of the highest
God, pull your inner strength and cross over to the new you, new
beginnings and new blessings"

"Challenges will always come and they are part of our daily
lives, that is why there is always victory at the end, but it is
determined by your inner strength. Let us always draw our
strength, when we feel weak. You are the only one who can draw
that strength or start to find excuses to your situation and shift
blames.

This will not help to shift blame, you cannot reverse what
happened but you can correct and learn from whatever situation
you have experienced.

All that I wish for you as my friend is the entire years to come,
enter them with peace, draw that strength, do not let or allow
darkness and negative thoughts to create you a comfort zone that
has fears, doubts and selfish behaviour and character. Isaiah 60:1
says 'Arise and shine, for the glory of the Lord has come' and Psalm
27:1 says 'the Lord is my light and my salvation; whom shall I fear?
The Lord is the strength of my life, of whom shall I be afraid? And
verse 14 of the same scriptures says "wait on the Lord, be of good
courage, and He shall strengthen your heart, wait; I say, on the
Lord, this is a weapon of faith"

"Never allow the people of this world dictate your potential,
your gift, press on and pursue it; it will be difficult and God never
said it will not, all that He said is to put our trust in Him,

If you can remember how we used to draw water in the olden days and using the old borehole pumping system that was installed for our usage in our villages, that is our life cycle, we use to wait patiently and queue, pump the system until the water comes out as a group/team, then depart by taking water to our home that is our destiny, when you get home, you will smile and sign because you have achieved the goal of getting the water you want for the family, you did it and with patience, and tomorrow was going to be the same routine and you will make it happen, that is life, facts and reality. All that we need, is patience, to pull our inner strength, whether hungry or not, pull that strength and do not give up. God will never give up on us and it not over until God says it is over, be a victorious warrior in all aspects of life"

"People told me I still look young and beautiful; *my answer is 'Cast your burdens, unto Jesus; for He cares for you..*

The other thing is my smile keeps me young and this beautiful smile"

"I do not wear clothes because they are very expensive, *I wear what suits me most, in particular for this gorgeous body' as long as it is also comfortable; whether it is less costly; one will not realise, what counts is the body shape and how the clothes fit; before the clothes, you identify is critical, your natural being is important, look stunning with or without a compliment" anyway you still look beautiful.*

"Never in your life, do something e.g. *Making yourself beautiful, buying clothes etc. to impress or seek someone admiration because you will get disappointed, if they do not recognise your efforts; rather do any of this to make yourself happy, fulfil the inner you! By doing this at your best for just for you; be happy with confidence even if none of spectators who are watching you* *do not appreciate what they see. Whatever you we, do, as long as you feel comfortable and satisfied, as longs as it brings out your confidence; feel free, that is you"*

"Never underestimate your success, *even if you can measure it as small, the fact of the matter is; you did it; never allow people to measure your success as nothing, rather find ways to achieve more, increase your success as if you are going to die tomorrow;*

All that I know is that; you know yourself more than any one, you can do it with or without anyone, your capabilities, potential starts from inside, the inner you, will reject or accept success; falling apart or failing is a step to self-realization, stand up and make a new plan to succeed, you are here on this earth for your purpose; talk to your Creator; He will make a way"

"Do not condemn yourself because of your yesterday mistakes, *your enemies are your steps to success, your failures is a lesson learnt, your downfall is a blessing in disguise"*

"Criticism and gossips makes you recognise *your presence in this world, it will promotes your achievements if you pull your socks up; these things completes your success and without them, you do not exists; be yourself"*

"It is bad when a person feels proud to make a negative impact in someone's career life, *especially if one is in a senior position to mentor, lead and coach. Take note that if your subordinate is incompetent, blame yourself first, do not use it against their weakness, one needs a change to improve through your assistant, you are there as a leader to impact positively into their lives" they still are intelligent unless you feel threatened and or intimidated"* *"**some people's ego issues can develop into jealousy** and it can hurt the innocent person's future"*

*"**We are appointed, elected to make changes as leaders,** to the disadvantaged because we are given this opportunity for a reason, one reason; to change the world; this is a privilege from above"*

*"**Never destroys someone's opportunity** because even yourself; someone out there is also waiting to destroy yours; you shall reap what you sow"*

*"**Before you can hurt someone**, put yourself into their shoes; your reward is coming"*

*"**Allow your instinct to guide you**; that is you conscious for the good" life is full of misery"*

*"**When you throw out someone out of their opportunities**, think about humanity, thinks of their debts, family they are responsible for, causing pain to someone is a bad investment with bad returns"*

*"**You are created to develop, inspires** and not to destroy; your power and or authority is temporary"*

*"**Do not ever live with regrets**, do the right things, the sooner the better to change your life and become proud of yourself"*

*"**Allow God's perfect will to take over** instead of our permissive will and either let Him find and know the desires of our hearts for His perfect will"*

"I always need His presence to teach, guide and lead me to feel comforted in times of sorrow; that is the Holy Spirit"

"challenges will shake me but not to be there to break me" I am still here so is you.

8

Finding Myself

F inding me was the best outcome of my survival in these challenges. Knowing that I have a purpose in this world, was the light that made me understand that I also have a special gift. That is inspiring people by sharing my story, the story of my past experiences.

I had to fight, to become bold, with courage to find time with myself, with God and ask Him what my purpose is. This was my gift to survive because I am still here and alive. I created myself a quiet place, a closet that I called an upper room in biblical term to do self-introspection review my potential, take note of how important I am in the lives of other people. This is my prayer and meditation place where I have a conversation with God about my life and where He is taking me.

I had to review the positive impact that I have made and the contributions that I have made in many people's lives to date and I could not count their appreciations. I had my secret place where I created a conversation with God, where my relationship with Him was spiritually elevated; He brought solutions to my situation including people who I counsel.

I was able to can read the word of God, my bible was inspiring me. I would be able to relate my story with men and woman in the bible and give myself hope. I had to learn to meditate and this became a therapy too. I had to learn to pray in truth and in spirit to reach out to God because it was between me and Him. I also became a worshipper. I am so blessed.

My bedroom changed to became my closet to stay in it, alone with powerful prayer and where I realised that I do not have to be a prisoner of my life but can be a president of my life. I had to release my spiritual gifts and stop torturing myself with anger and bitterness. I had to forget that I was once exploited because if I cannot move out of this cycle of depression, I was not even realising that I have a gift that can connect me to the world of peace with expectations to my Creator.

We do fight with our gift that is why we become so unhappy in the long run if we do not know what kind of a gift we are having. We are all born with different gifts, gifts that can also survive us economically. When you use your gift effectively, you will become happy with peace and you will definitely become successful because your gift is your purpose.

The other thing is that you need to pray to find and connect with the relevant people who will identify, nourish and support your gift without exploiting it and or abusing it for their own benefits.

I am blessed because I was privileged to find my gift, something that I am capable of, sharing my story in a form of writing, preaching and motivating people was the best gifts ever that was hidden by the shadow of emotional traumas.

The best outcome that fulfils me, is the response of my audience, how I connected with them and my individual one on one session with women, children and men is always amazing. This has confirmed that I am in the right path of living my purpose. The presence of the Holy Spirit when I ascend the stage to show me a sign that God is with me, makes me to want more of sharing to the multitude from nations to nations, how God is in my life. This makes me a happy person and also very important. This is my purpose, to stand in front of people and talk my experience and my testimonies to their challenges, to give the courage and hope that they can also make it in life because I also did it.

Your gift can fight with you if you do not allow it to be used and known effectively. You can also have depression if you do not use it. You are not fulfilled emotionally, physically and psychologically. That is a life, full of frustration and misery until you realise it. The environment can reject you, even where you work or where you are involved without using your gift can be unsatisfying, even when people do not understand your gift, can make you unfulfilled. It is important to find yourself, make yourself happy by knowing what is your gift that you are born with, and not only a gift but the primary gift that can also survives you and connect you to the world.

As parents, we need to help, support and engage our children to know and understand their gifts at the early age. That is our key responsibility for the successful future of our children. Observe and communicate with them effective until they explore and know what they want to show case their gift.

I have realised my gift at the late adult stage because my parents were not educated as much as to can fulfil my expectations to observe and realise my gift. My mother would know but couldn't do much, she gave me the liberty to explore for myself and it was not easy. I use to share my spiritual dreams with her and she would interpret them for the direction to where God was taking me and sometimes I wouldn't agree with her, but today more of the visions that I shared with her are happening.

I remember before she passed on, she told me to read the book of Job and I perceived she was referring to herself only to find out at the later stage that it was her prophesy to me, I will go through financial struggle and lose my house etc. but that God will restore after these experience. I can now consider my gift and my siblings' gifts seriously, because in the past, it was all about socio-economic survival more than our growth and our gift to explore, as individuals in the family. All that I know more about us is that we can all sing, worship and praise to get to another level of our spiritual fulfilment.

I am blessed that I am here for my kids, that I also mentor and sister's kids. All that I want is for you to have self-realisation moment, find out what is your gift, it has never been late to do that, age for me has no impact at all. Healthy lifestyle counts more, taking care of yourself and making you happy is the best outcome of all.

Forgiving, loving and caring for me first have made me to transfer these elements of life to my family, neighbour and to anyone who I meet. I have created the chain of love to those who are close to me. That is the mark that I want to leave behind.

You cannot move on IF you do not forgive yourself and others. Stop becoming a prisoner of your past and unlock your potential.

'Criticism is full of elevation; the question is…Can YOU do better if criticised?

Judgement is a promotion; the question is …are YOU perfect? No, no one in this entire world is perfect…stop beating up yourself to please or prove to the world that you can be perfect. Do it for you and people will always judge you doing right or wrong things…it never ends

I have found myself and the world has found me as perfect as I am, there was no need to listen to their criticism and judgement but I was supposed to have focused on what I want, what makes me happy and what I need to fulfil my dreams. To teach them who I am without allowing them to pull me down… but to show or be the best that I can be…life is too short to fill it with regrets. I am about to celebrate my life to the best. I am what God says I AM. I want to have a significant journey where I will learn and live.

Finding me inside out, is not about getting married or having kids and or looking at my age as a threat, but to know and understand the inner me, the potential and fulfilment of peace inside of me that counts most.

My family sees many positive reactions and approaches in my life when I am in social activities; they know I am a survivor and that I will always strive for success. With regard to marriage and kids, I do have kids, my sisters children are my kids… I have young people around the world who admires my mentorship and coaching style and they are my children too. I have male friends who make me feel special.

I do not have to think of intimacy or sex knowing that I am not ready and the husband is not there yet, but I know when the right time will come to have it responsibly, I will but with the right person and at the right time without regrets, just being in control of what I am doing and the temptations thereof.

Young people do sexual activities in the dark and do not want to be matured to act responsible because there is consequences to account to from doing that, some do not know why they are doing it, and the outcome of that is depression and misery. Act responsible with accountabilities but note that your happiness and future goals come first and you need to prioritise that, you have the whole authority to your success, it is not about your social background or your parents, they can die in your eyes and you can be left behind to face the reality of life. It is a must, because you are still young, to dream of becoming a change to your family and community. Do not get influenced easily, know what you want, control your feelings, change you mind-set and make yourself happy with positive things and friends.

What I am currently enjoying is the positive impact that I am doing by travelling around my area sharing my story and the positive response that I am getting after my presentations and motivations. What I like most is when I motivate women in churches, youth and church members including one on one counselling sessions after every tour.

I am not doing it for money but helping other people to realise that there is hope in every season that we go through. It has also been a cure and a therapy to my soul and my spirit.

I will always believe that I had to go through what I have experienced to tell a story, that will heal the broken hearts and note that they cannot reverse what happened in their past, but can press on to become better. We can all have a new life that I call abundant restoration of greener pastures after every situation that we encounter and overcome. we have to be overcomers, we need to conquer because our strength is drawn within us and we need to maintain it with prayer.

I feel privileged that I can change someone's life through my different experiences. I believe I am this unique light that can bring a smile to someone, when there is darkness in their life. I do not fear judgement to what has happened to me when I share story, because it is the past; unless someone can be brave and be able to judge me of my present and future life. I am stubborn to criticism because I know what I want and where I am going.

I know I will face seasons of difficulties in the future, but the foundation of my courage is that; I have overcome my past and has allowed my inner strength to work for me to date.

I know that I do not have to be educated and rich to make a difference or positive impact in someone's life. That is not the only thing but this is an additional to what you were born with, your natural intelligent and how perfect you were created count most. All that I need is for you to care as much as you can. I know it is in me to be kind and to be there for my family as a sister and a friend. That is my natural intelligence and how significant I can be.

For me to feel important is when people reminded me of my value in their lives, to express their frustrations bringing solutions with wisdom and guidance from the Holy Spirit is important to me. This has brought revival and strength to them, and also using the word of God. This is my gift and that is where I become more fulfilled. Standing in front of people and encouraging them also becomes a fulfilment.

I do admirer people who have experienced tough times in their past life, and still prevail as victors. I am one of them and will prevail. God is the author and the finisher and or the perfecter of my faith and I truly trust Him.

One thing that I have realized is that I am more beautiful than before and my secret of becoming more younger is my relationship with God, my prayerful life, making myself happy through thick and thin, inspiring people by sharing my story, eating healthy, ongoing forgiveness, smiling even if it is too hard to do so, admiring my image, my beauty before people can say it or compliment me.

All that I can say is…find your purpose, realise your potential, know your gifts and prioritise them. The gift that you are born with will survive you financially. It will lead you to become successful citizen in your country.

Do not ever live under the shadow of someone's life and success, have your own successful story. It causes a delay and can lead to depression when you realises that you have wasted time to please someone out there who did not appreciate and respect you. You will always feel used and to get your independent life back is a huge work and it can drain you emotionally.

I have learnt to communicate my expectations to anyone I make contact with or have to partner with; it is take or leave it. I am very conscientious to look for signs of rejections and accept things that I cannot change and or have authority over them. I always have a room for disappointment and my inner peace has helped a lot.

I have been disappointed by many people even when I was raising funds for my books, many people did not take me serous when I told them I have written these books.

I was laughing with one of my friend and my family that the perception of my depression has not yet faded away. People still think I am depressed when I told them I have written books. It is still disbelief to them but this is a testimony for me and to the world.

This is not stopping me from pursuing the publication and the launching process of my books and I am busy writing more books. This was and is my goal to achieve with or without any help or favour of any person. I am going to achieve more.

I had to trust my instinct and I always believe that God will approve and give permission to people who will support me in any initiative that I embark on. God will also give permission to my husband to find me and see me as his wife and a rib. Find who you are and what makes you happy. God is always on time for everything that you do, it is not about people but it is between you and God.

Teach people to love, care and understand the real you. Do not live a fake life and pretend to be someone you are not. God has chosen and created people who will tolerate, compromise with patience and efforts, to understand the real you without judging you. I have found such people who sometimes will be honest to have a constructive criticism to what I am doing with love and care. Their approach to correct me will connect with my emotions and my soul. My family are also free to do that, I told them it is an obligation for them to help me and tell me when I am off ramping from the good side of me.

The people that God choses in your life will be there and honest without back biting you. They will also suggest better solutions in their approach with support measures. They will never pull you down. I do have such people and we end up laughing about every achievement from what we deliberated on; to build to any of my idea. We sometimes ignore people who are meant to advise us because of their status and position or social background. Ordinary people counts when it comes to giving good advice.

Learn to love, associate with any kind of people, race and colour, and age; you will meet the best people who will support your dreams without judging you. There is always new season ahead of our future experiences and every season has its own consequences, be ready for any change in every season of your life.

I have learnt to know what is wrong before I can judge anyone. I have been perceived wrong, I have been criticized that I do not have qualifications etc. I was told I do not qualify to what certain people believed I was incapable of but God took me to another level of success to understand my gift and my unknown potential. God intervened and qualified me when I was disqualified by the world.

It starts with me, I am the president of my life, I am the CEO of my life, my household, and I can be a CEO to any company.

I do not regard people as unemployed, I always say to them "They are the executive of their potential, their gift, they can direct it if they pursue themselves to success. Their gift can bring income and they can become employers through their gift, we all need to know and understand our gift and make it alive"

My song now is "It was not easy but it is worth it", I AM SHARING THIS STORY BECAUSE I SURVIVED.

I went out of my comfort zone, I even sold my house after struggling financially trying this and that to pay it, for about five years, unemployed, applying for a job, trying business with no avail, that I nearly lost my house for auction. My house became a investment to another investment before I could lose it totally without the return and I had to go back home and live in my mother's house.

I met strangers that I call angels who survived me financially to keep my house financially stable until I was able to sell it and not to lose it completely with nothing in return. These strangers never expect anything but I call them angels of my season of struggle who were send by God, to rescue me till I had decided on the best solution ever. I had a financial provision that gave me more time to think deeply and accept that I need to sell my house. It was not easy but today I found many positive reasons why I had to sell my house.

My first reason was the peace that I felt after selling it, the peace that I felt after moving back home and the full time support that I got from my sisters and brother in laws. They even thought I would have another attack of Depression when I was selling my house and they were amazed how I reacted positively towards the process. I spoke with God and He gave me peace with successful promises I can call.

I had to become a living testimony from all my challenges. An overcome of situations after situations, standing bold and believe that I will definitely become successful. I do not fear anything including death, I have seen it all and I survived. God still sustained me, because I still have a purpose.

I loved my house, never thought that I could sell it so quickly, it was an investment but I still had many plans to do more to it before I could even think of selling it. I had to, in my heart these comforting words came now and then that "God's plan and thought are not mine" anything happens for a reason.

I did not have a choice to lose it for with nothing in return. I had to sell at reasonable price, before the bank can take it through sheriff. I had God send people to facilitate the process quickly within the duration that the bank gave me. I was able to pay the areas before I could sell it. Thanks to my perfect angels.

This house was my last investment and I thank God that it survived me. It gave me the returns on investment that assisted me to pay all my debts including all people who I owe. I was able to fix my car, renovated my late mom's house that I currently live in and the rest went back to investing on my 3 books.

I have not raised my expectation in getting more revenue for these books as a priority to my return on my investment. I am at peace because writing these books was a blessing and huge therapy to me, to heal, inspire people that through all these experiences.

I am still here given the privilege and honour, to tell my story and the rest shall follow on how they sell themselves, is in God's hands. He had made it possible for me to make me write them and to pay for them so that they can become published. That is all that counts.

I am moving forward to my new life, starting afresh, Debts free, new investments, renewed with peace, new beginning, new season of joy, laughter, family bonding like never before. I wake up every morning full of worship and praise, with thanks giving. I have learnt to praise Him in do and out do season. This is my strength to overcome. He is providing daily for me as if I am employed.

"Success can be achieved where you less expected, you can lose something valuable at your heart not knowing the sacrifice of losing that thing…can open other, many doors of success"

LIFE IS A RISK, IT HAS TOMORROW WITH THINGS UNTOLD, THAT CAN UNFOLD NEGETIVELY OR POSITIVELY, BUT TO REACH OUT TO THEM, IT NEEDS COURAGE, THERE ARE THINGS UNTOLD, BUT DREAMS TO ACHIEVE CAN CONNECT WITH YOU, BE DIRECTED TO YOU, LOCATE WITH YOU… AMAZING TO CALL THEM TESTIMONY

I made it to have ISBN, for three books, hopefully more to come…I AM AT PEACE…ENJOYING LIFE..

9

Acknowledgement

This message is for this young man when he was age of 5, when I was going through depression "you were a child but became a best friend, very protective and always reminded me of how much God loves me, that I will always be amazed by the words of your encouragement that came out of your young, innocent mouth. You were there for me 24hrs even reminding your parents that I need to be taken care of. I know I will always be the best rich Mmamogolo in your hopes and eyes; As you always told me that I have millions and millions of money" I quote.

My late mom 'Angel in Heaven, I survived. I always wish you can see me and be there every time I stand in front of the crowd especially when there is standing ovation, thinking how will you feel and imagine your tears of being proud of your little girl. I will always feel you in my heart when I approach the stage always… because you believed in me that I will make it in future"

Thanks to the members of my family, my four (4) sisters, all my nephews and nieces, brothers in law, relatives, friends, former colleagues, family friends who I have learnt from their experiences, and who I shared my experiences with on one on one basis. Some have inspired me and they were a therapy during my tough seasons. Some do not even know that they were my blessing; but they will know when they read my books. I really appreciate each and every word that they said to me that I tool it serious; even some didn't know what I was going through but they did make a positive impact during my depression season. I was and am blessed to have met all of you.

I pass my sincere thanks to all the pastors, women and men of God who I have met, for their spiritual prayers and inspirational words that made a positive *impact in my life, together with their congregations. It was not easy but it was worth it.*

All Radio stations that gave me the opportunity to share with me their lifestyle and reality shows. I appreciate that they did allow me to present my inspirations and motivation with viewers. Thanks to community leaders who gave me the opportunity in their events to become their motivational guest speaker *and believed in my potential to date.*

Lastly, to all the people who saw a need to bless me financially, when I was in need without sharing my situation but they continue to plant a seed because God did touch them as angels to assist me. He will definitely bless you abundantly, above, beyond measures until the cup of your blessings overflows.

I am very thankful that God gave me a chance to live, a chance to proof to myself that I am able, to make the impossible; possible, to open doors of success for me and close the doors of failure. I THANK MY LATE MOTHER FOR HER BELIEVE SYSTEM, HER FAITH IN THE LORD JESUS CHRIST WHO ALSO SAVED ME.

Above all, the Almighty God who sustained me throughout these challenge to find my purpose.

10

Biography

Pauline Magauta Molokwane

Born *1972, born and lives in Phokeng-Rustenburg-North West Province- South Africa*

17yrs, ***work experience****, specialize in Community/youth Development work, Project Management, Business Development and Strategies, Stakeholder Relations and Counselling.*

Diploma in Youth Development *with University of South Africa*

Certificates *in Project Management with X-pert Group Academy South Africa*

Certificate *in Management Development Programme (MAP) with Wits Business School*

Likes *cooking, gardening, travelling, music, reading, doing poetry, write and a Motivational Speaker in schools, churches, Community events, Women events, Youth events, Corporate company events and radio stations,*

Currently unemployed and willing to pursue my career for extra income, to study Psychology and acquire my MBA and will continue to write books, catering and selling nutritional products.

SPORTS; Tennis, athletics, swimming.

Personality: Extrovert, hard work, perfectionist, loving, kind and caring, generous, ambitious.

Facebook page – *Pauline Magauta Molokwane*

Contacts – *0790158878 or 0818712986*

Email *address:* *paulinemagauta@gmail.com*

www.magauta-mylifejourney.com